# Junior Faculty Development: A Handbook

*Donald K. Jarvis*

THE MODERN LANGUAGE ASSOCIATION OF AMERICA
NEW YORK, NY    1991

© 1991 by The Modern Language Association of America

**Library of Congress Cataloging-in-Publication Data**

Jarvis, Donald K., 1939–
 Junior faculty development: a handbook / Donald K. Jarvis
  p.  cm.
 ISBN 0-87352-383-0  ISBN 0-87352-384-9 (pbk.)
 1. College teachers—United States.  I. Title.
LB1778.2.J37 1991
378.1'2'0973—dc20   91-12823


Second printing 1992

Published by The Modern Language Association of America
10 Astor Place, New York, New York 10003-6981

*To Janelle—*
*a dedicated mentor*

# CONTENTS

# PREFACE

MOST PROFESSORS ASSUME that the last two decades' extensive literature on faculty development includes a reasonable amount of advice on helping junior faculty members. Unfortunately, it does not. Since the middle of the 1970s many authors have discussed faculty development, but they have mostly been concerned with aging and tenured faculty members, viewing junior professors merely as the answer to an excess of senior faculty members. That view is naive: junior faculty members may be less likely to be tired and cynical, but they have their own challenges and weaknesses. Most of them report that they are under daunting pressures and very much need help.

This book is based on the premises that even the best junior faculty members can benefit from assistance and that investments in junior faculty development are a wise use of university resources. Each faculty member costs the university over a million dollars during a thirty-five-year career, so it makes good business sense to try to enhance the return on that investment. As chapter 1 points out, however, the main reasons for assisting junior professors are not just monetary but humane and practical.

This book is intended to encourage and assist senior faculty members— including appointed university and college leaders—in establishing both institutional and informal development programs for junior professors. It can also serve as a self-help guide for junior and senior faculty members at a variety of institutions, from junior colleges to prominent research institutions, and as a guide for job seekers who want to evaluate academic institutions offering employment.

Readers will find here incentives, evaluation techniques, and model programs for developing not only sound research and writing habits but also the arts of good teaching and institutional citizenship. My recommendations are based on a review of the general fields of personnel and faculty development, augmented by study of several established programs for junior faculty development and by over one hundred interviews conducted with researchers, teachers, and administrators in the humanities.

This guide touches only briefly on questions of graduate training, since that subject has been widely discussed elsewhere. I do not consider the issue of junior faculty recruiting, to which Bowen and Schuster have devoted an entire chapter. Furthermore, this guide does not summarize the extensive literature on college-level teaching methods or on the problems of part-time teachers and graduate teaching assistants.

Readers may focus on a specific aspect of junior faculty development by simply turning to the appropriate chapter. Chapter 3 is strongly recommended for all readers, however, because it surveys fundamental questions of evaluation and reward methods. The first section of chapter 5 is also important, because it reviews the basics of faculty development. Readers already convinced of the value of junior faculty development might want to skip to chapter 7 for an overview of the essentials in a junior faculty development program and then work back through the chapters most interesting to them.

Chapter 1 outlines the rationale for junior faculty development, sketching both short- and long-run benefits for institutions and faculty members.

Chapter 2 presents the thesis that the criteria for promotion and tenure should be carefully considered to enhance long-term university interests, which tend to coincide with faculty interests. The relative weight of publication, teaching, and university service varies from institution to institution, but most departments want to ensure that their faculty members represent a variety of interests and skills.

Chapter 3 discusses methods for evaluating and rewarding faculty members. The differences among scholarship, research, and publication are noted, along with the extensive literature on evaluating teaching. The chapter takes into account both tangible and intangible rewards.

Chapter 4 reviews the importance of the junior professor's dossier in the tenure and promotion process, suggests types of data that it could include, and recommends several principles for assembling a convincing and effective document.

Chapter 5 surveys programs for developing good research and publication skills and emphasizes the role of collegiality—the mentoring, networking, and support that provide young professors with the sense of being part of a lively community of scholars. This chapter also reviews key findings from the intellectual autobiographies of our interview subjects.

Chapter 6 suggests how to help young faculty members develop their teaching. It surveys teaching-oriented programs together with the crucial principles of administrative and peer support. This chapter's basic premise is that teaching and publication are subsets of a single whole—the conversation of a community of scholars.

Chapter 7 discusses ways of appropriately involving junior faculty members in university service.

Chapter 8 presents two model junior faculty development programs: one represents the absolute minimum that must be done; the other is an ideal program for those institutions that have the will and the means to attain excellence.

Chapter 9 summarizes the preceding chapters and discusses implications for future study.

Appendix 1 contains a selected list of publications helpful to those interested in junior faculty development.

Appendix 2 lists information about organizations involved in the subject.

Appendix 3 reproduces the questionnaire used in the interview project described below.

Appendix 4 details the results of our survey of scholars, teachers, administrators, and junior faculty members.

This project developed out of my five-year assignment in the office of the dean of general education at Brigham Young University. Our efforts to improve the general-education program led us back again and again to faculty development and recruitment. A brief look at the demographics of our faculty convinced us that nearly half of the members would need to be replaced within fifteen years, so we would soon need to handle a large influx of junior professors. I began looking for means of helping these professors develop in ways that would benefit both them and the university.

I collected a small research group in 1986, and we began studying junior faculty development issues. We were surprised at the lack of pertinent literature and decided that original research was needed. It seemed to us that those best qualified to comment on the subject would be successful senior professors and a few select junior professors.

We interviewed over one hundred influential faculty members at eight universities and colleges in the United States: the University of Chicago, Dickinson College, Harvard University, the University of California at Santa Cruz, the University of Illinois at Chicago, the University of Maryland at College Park, Stanford University, and Yale University. We chose Santa Cruz and Dickinson because of their reputations as institutions concerned about good teaching; Maryland and Illinois because they are typical large public institutions; and the rest because of their acknowledged excellence in scholarship, confirmed by study of publications in the *Arts and Humanities Citation Index*. We selected most of our informants from the humanities, an area almost totally neglected in the work on faculty research productivity. Once again we consulted the *Arts and Humanities Citation Index*, first identifying the scholars who had published the most frequently over the past decade and then finding those who had been recently cited the most frequently by others. The names of teachers and administrators for our study were provided by deans of arts and sciences or comparable administrators.

Most interviews lasted thirty to sixty minutes and were conducted in the faculty member's office, although a very few were done by telephone. Following expert advice, I did not use a tape recorder but took handwritten notes that I entered into a computer each evening. The interview form is reproduced in appendix 3, and the number and types of faculty members interviewed at each institution are listed in appendix 4.

Toward the end of the project, we felt the need for more sophisticated and experienced advice on improving teaching. I therefore visited the Central Pennsylvania Consortium and spent a morning interviewing the principal organizers of its long-running junior faculty development program. I also interviewed by telephone seven administrators who had organized local or national programs in the Lilly Endowment's Teaching Fellows program. I telephoned three individuals involved with the Joyce Foundation's shared-professorship program at Beloit College. Finally I joined the Professional and Organizational Development Network in Higher Education, attended its annual conferences, and read its publications.

When I began this project, few were paying attention to junior faculty members, but that situation has changed drastically. Perhaps this volume and subsequent works will make a difference for some young professionals and those they teach. In any case, writing this book for my junior colleagues has made me a better senior professor, an effect that illustrates a curious constant in the mentoring business.

# ACKNOWLEDGMENTS

THE COLLEGE OF HUMANITIES and the Office of Academic Vice President of Brigham Young University provided generous financial support for this project as it evolved from its original focus on faculty research productivity to more general questions of faculty development. I am indebted to BYU colleagues Gene W. Dalton, Keith Warner, Howard M. Bahr, and Phillip Kunz, all of whom read through data and early proposals, offered advice, and helped a bumbling humanist learn something of social-science research. I am further grateful to the following individuals, who all read through final versions of the manuscript and made helpful suggestions: Robert Boice of the State University of New York at Stony Brook; Douglas Gomery of the University of Maryland; my wife, Janelle Jamison Jarvis; and Brigham Young University colleagues Michelle Stott, Howard Christie, Bryan J. Fogg, Andi Reese, and John S. Harris. Of course, any deficiencies in the manuscript are my responsibility.

Jennifer Stone and Michael F. Peterson served as efficient typists and research assistants. Vaughn Peterson provided critical help and served as my main research assistant, critic, and adviser during his busy final year in a graduate program in organizational behavior. Most important were the faculty members whom I visited at the eight institutions and who graciously gave of their time, thought, and humor to help with this project.

# CHAPTER 1

# The Case for Junior Faculty Development

## Genghis Khan on Promotion and Tenure

PROFESSOR HORATIA STRIVER was irritated. She had been trapped on the wrong side of the water fountain by Earnest Plummer—the busybody dean of faculty at Heartland State University—who was subjecting her to a sales pitch on something called "junior faculty envelopment." It sounded like a harebrained educationist's program and was sure to be a waste of time and money. She was a busy professional—full professor of comparative literature, chair of the Committee on Promotion and Tenure, and member of the faculty senate—and, under the gun to finish an article by the end of the week, she was eager to return to the real world of her word processor. But Plummer kept saying something about "a threat to the quality we've worked for," and he was exercised enough that Horatia thought she ought to appear interested.

"So who are you talking about, Ernie? What do you mean by junior faculty? Anyone who is not a full professor, or what?"

Plummer replied, "Actually, I mean any full-time faculty members who don't have tenure yet. Most of them have been here less than eight years and know that within six or so years, we will decide whether to grant tenure or ask them to leave."[1]

"And what is this program of envelopment?"

"Not envelopment, *development*," answered the dean, a little impatiently.

"Oh, yes—teaching improvement."

"No, Horatia, definitely not just teaching improvement. *Development* designates any effort to improve the performance of faculty members as researchers, teachers, or citizens of a local community of scholars. We're talking about a well-balanced approach."

"So who does it to whom?" asked Striver warily. She had read enough Lenin to know the right questions to ask about institutional power. "This is something the administration does to unsuspecting young professors, right?"

"Development is not just something that the administration does to the faculty, or older professors to younger ones," Plummer explained. "It's the personal growth that all academics should be engaged in all the time, or at least should feel guilty about if they are not. It means self-improvement as well as institutional programs."

"Well, Ernie, no one could oppose junior faculty development if you define it like that. That's like home, mother, and apple pie. The issue is how much *collective* responsibility we are willing to accept as institutions and colleagues. I, for one, believe in the sink-or-swim approach to development: hire a bunch of energetic kids, throw them into the mainstream, stand back, and see who can swim."

"Well, yes," answered Plummer, a bit pained. "For the most part, junior faculty development has been a matter of institutions raising their standards and the junior professors doing their own developing as best they could. In the clear employers' market of the 1970s and 1980s, American institutions could select the best among many excellent candidates and give them each a full teaching load, a few administrative chores, and three to six years in which to produce significant publications. Most institutions put the burden almost entirely on the junior faculty members, and many schools discouraged cooperation among young recruits by hiring several to compete for each permanent position. If an untenured teacher performed any function inadequately, the responsible thing was simply to fire that person and hire someone else."

"You'd better believe it. That's how you raise quality. The P and T committee has had a lot of fights with the English department, which is always feeling sorry for nice people with inadequate publication records and trying to sneak them by. But if the department ends up with a bunch of duds to carry for the next thirty years, everybody suffers."

"So you would agree with the ancient wisdom that 'regret is the fruit of pity'?" asked Plummer.

"Exactly. Great quote. Who said it?"

"Genghis Khan."

"You play hardball, don't you?" observed Striver cheerfully. She had beaten Plummer at enough arguments that she could afford to grant him a point now and then. "OK, but universities cannot coddle the indolent and incompetent. We have an obligation to our students to maintain or raise our standards, and the responsibility for development rests on the individual professor. We have tight budgets and need to be tough-minded about where we put our resources. We can't be trapped by ivory-tower idealism—we must be, well, businesslike. Top managers in the business world put the good of the organization first and fire employees that don't measure up. They're not bleeding hearts who waste a lot of money and time on the development of their employees. There it's a rat race with 'every man for himself, and the devil take the hindmost.'"

Plummer smelled another easy point but started off diplomatically. "You're certainly right that the business community puts the good of the organization first. But, strangely enough, management's view of what's best for the organization seems more and more to include the welfare of the *employees.* American businesses spend enormous sums in helping their employees make successful careers. For instance, IBM currently invests $500 million annually in education and training [Brown]. A Carnegie Foundation report found that the amount American businesses spend each year on education and development of their employees roughly equals the total budgets of all the colleges and universities in the United States [Eurich 6]. And I've heard the Japanese corporations do even more for employee development than our companies do."

"You're kidding. Businesses spend as much on the education of their employees as the regular academic establishment does on that of its paying clientele, the students? Incredible."

"But true. By comparison, American institutions of higher learning do very little to develop their employees in any organized way and do even less to help junior faculty members. The Carnegie Foundation's head, Ernest Boyer, claims that budgeting for faculty development is rare [134], and experts like John Centra rate most faculty development programs as poor at reaching those who need them most [153]. Hardly anything is done in the first year after hiring to help professors improve their teaching [Fink, *First Year* 106–07]. Jack Schuster, who knows the American professoriat as well as anyone does, sums up the situation by saying that as employers, 'colleges would rarely deserve a grade as high as D for what they do for their instructional staff' [Watkins]."

## Demographics Rears Its Ugly Head

"All right, Ernie," Striver said, "so maybe we don't do too much to help either junior or senior faculty members, but we have plenty of new professors to choose from. Our way may not be altruistic, but at least our institutional quality is up."

"True enough, Horatia, but the old methods don't work when supply is tight. We have been blindsided by a shift in faculty demographics: many of our faculty members were hired in the 1950s and 1960s, are now well over fifty, and will retire before or soon after the year 2000. Some writers started worrying about this trend in the mid-eighties [Bowen and Schuster 198], then the *Chronicle* ran some articles about how colleges are trying to cope with the coming faculty shortage [Mooney], and in 1989 the Mellon Foundation funded a careful look at faculty supply and demand [Bowen and Sosa]."

"And what did they find?" asked Striver.

"Well, they didn't see any sharp bunching of retirements coming up, and they saw the crunch coming a little later, but their general conclusions were at least as ominous as the earlier ones: beginning at the end of the 1990s, demand for professors would exceed supply, especially in the humanities and social sciences, where they predicted that only seven candidates would be found for every ten jobs [Bowen and Sosa]."

"Any local evidence of all this?"

"Plenty. Not only have my staff been getting more positions to fill, but it is receiving fewer applications than normal because the poor job markets in the 1970s and 1980s caused a plunge in the numbers of students earning PhDs in many fields.[2] To complicate matters, graduates are taking longer to earn their doctorates: in 1967 they averaged only 5.4 years, but by 1987 they were stretching it out to nearly 7 years [Evangelauf]. Moreover, a dramatic increase in two-career families has further reduced the mobility of potential applicants and hence narrowed our options. Perhaps most worrisome of all is the evidence that a smaller proportion of the most talented young students are opting for academic careers [Bowen and Schuster 225–30]. As a result, our chairs will have less choice when hiring in the next decade, and even with careful selection many will have difficulty maintaining quality. I think we have the same situation here that you see across the country, and all of us at Heartland will be forced to do more with our in-service programs to sustain and improve the quality of our faculty."

"The Henny Pennys are usually wrong," countered Horatia. "I haven't been recruiting lately, but the last time we hired we had plenty of applicants. Besides, what about the new retirement laws? Some people are going to want to stay on longer. Won't that soften the crunch?"

"The Mellon study says no. Looking at our situation, I tend to agree. In a few cases delaying retirement may help somewhat, but at best the crunch will just be postponed a few years, no more than five. The basic supply-and-demand problem won't be solved."

## The Fateful First Job

"Besides," Plummer continued, "even if the quantity and quality of applicants weren't problems, there would still be plenty of compelling reasons to establish programs for developing and motivating new faculty members. If an institution decides that extensive scholarly publishing is essential to achieving tenure, then common sense and decency suggest that academic leaders help junior professors find the time, resources, and collegiality critical to establishing early habits of scholarship. Did you know that several studies indicate that professors' first places of employment have more influence on their careers than their graduate schools do?"[3]

That shook Striver, a proud alumna of Ivymoney University. "The first job has more effect on the career than the graduate school does?"

"That's what the evidence shows. Unfortunately, few institutions provide the help commensurate with their expectations of junior professors, and a lot of talented people are wasted. Because of an oversupply of excellent applicants during the 1970s, employers could afford to give new faculty members large teaching loads, to leave them to their own devices, and then to fire those who did not meet the rigorous publishing standards. There was some grousing about how faculty loyalty to the institution had dropped unconscionably, but in an employers' market, most good institutions could get away with what I call the 'Kleenex approach': use 'em and throw 'em away. Now it's clear that most of us will have to live with the junior faculty members we hire, and they will become our senior faculty. If the university is the faculty, then the junior faculty is the university's future."

"So you are saying that if we want to maintain quality, we're going to have to demand a bit less and help our junior faculty members more, now that we have fewer applicants for more slots?" asked Professor Striver.

## Walking and Chewing Gum at the Same Time

"That's part of it," replied the dean. "Of course, another issue is the criteria by which junior faculty members are judged. Many academic leaders who are humane and provide young professors the time to develop a reasonable balance of skill in research, teaching, and institutional service find themselves losing excellent faculty members because the local tenure and promotion standards overemphasize publication, while virtually ignoring teaching and service. Eloquent tribute is usually paid to the last two, but at most big universities they aren't evaluated with enough care to play a serious role in tenure and promotion decisions. It's as though we can't walk and chew gum at the same time. It's not true, it's silly, and it's counterproductive."

Striver had been through this emotional issue so many times that she hurried to agree. "No argument. We not only have to help develop and evaluate research skills in our new people: we need to work on their teaching skills too."

"Right." The dean pressed on, explaining, "Even if reward criteria are balanced and congruent with long-term institutional goals, a good share of our new professors are narrowly specialized and poorly prepared to teach undergraduates. They might be salvaged by the right help at the right time, but some excellent researchers are discarded because of their inept teaching—or, even worse, are retained to teach below their potential during much of their careers. If we are going to maintain quality in research and teaching around here, we have to pay more attention to junior faculty development."

## The Big Question: Will Development Programs Help?

Striver could see that what the dean had in mind would cost time and money, and she was worried. She knew that her university budget was austere already. "I doubt the value of professional development programs for faculty members in general and for junior professors in particular. To me, the word *development* conjures up a meddlesome administration that views the faculty as doddering, in need of remediation or perhaps early retirement. Having bothered the senior faculty for a decade or so, the do-gooders now aim to inflict themselves on the hapless junior faculty. I agree with Thoreau's view of people out to do good: 'If I knew for a certainty that a man was coming to my house with the conscious design of doing me good, I should run for my life . . .' [55]. The junior faculty members I know are for the most part bright, energetic, and capable of getting along without a lot of well-meaning interference."

"Eloquently put, Horatia, as usual," conceded Dean Plummer. "Certainly our junior professors seem more energetic and capable than most of our senior professors. Agreed that a few rugged individualists may not want help, but they represent a small minority. For one thing, untenured faculty members today are under far more stress than were those who entered higher education before 1970, when publication was less important. Bowen and Schuster conclude that junior professors often endure a 'grueling and lonely ordeal' [149]. Two researchers studied new faculty members at a typical large regional university on the West Coast and found that 85% reported significant job-related stress [Turner and Boice, "Starting"]. Another writer found about the same thing in the Midwest [Sorcinelli].

"Finally," continued Plummer, trying not to bore his audience, "you have to admit that junior faculty development rests on exactly the same premise as does our whole educational enterprise—belief in the value of a cooperative rather than a purely individualistic approach to learning. Professors and all other professional educators base their hope of employment on a commitment to working together to learn. This belief in cooperation alongside individual effort is accepted at all levels from kindergarten through graduate school and, in the last two decades, has been extended to senior faculty members as well. The junior faculty level, neglected because of the recent employers' market, is now an anomalous stage in which young people are temporarily left more to their own devices than they ever were before or will be again if granted tenure."

## Conclusion, at Last

"If I understand what you are trying to say, Ernie, you admit you cannot prove that junior faculty development always works for everyone, but you think you have scored the following points in your quaint, deanly way:

- The cost-conscious business community invests incredible sums in employee development.
- Fluctuating quantity and quality of graduate enrollments mean that future job-applicant pools will not always contain the merits that academic leaders desire.
- The first employment position apparently plays a disproportion-ately influential role in a professor's career.
- Academic institutions must ensure that their selection criteria encourage a balance of research and teaching excellence.
- Junior professors seem to appreciate the development programs so far established.
- Junior faculty development programs rest on exactly the same premise—the value of cooperation—as does the whole educational establishment.

What have I missed?"

"Not a particle, as usual," purred Plummer, pleased with his propaganda. "Junior faculty development is at least a good risk, if not one of the most important tasks for people who care about the university. Faculty quality is the main index of university quality, and the junior faculty represents the future of the university. Only a decreasing number of the wealthiest research universities can continue to play the parasite, exploiting and neglecting their own junior faculties and then hiring excellent senior scholars who have developed elsewhere. Of course, even the best development program will not guarantee that all junior professors will succeed, but for the good of the whole academic enterprise, we should offer a program to help them.

Undaunted, Professor Striver snatched victory from the jaws of defeat. "Approve my doctoral program in comp. lit. and I'll see if I can swing a few votes in the faculty senate when your proposal comes up."

"Talk about *me* playing hardball," grumbled the dean.

## NOTES

[1] This decision is referred to colloquially as "up or out," since an offer of tenure is often connected with a promotion in rank. Junior faculty members typically hold the rank of instructor, assistant professor, or occasionally even associate professor, and they usually have either earned a doctoral degree or completed all the requirements for it except writing a dissertation. The terms *junior faculty member* and *junior professor* are usually interchangeable and in this book are also synonymous with designations *new* and *inexperienced* applied to *professor, researcher, teacher,* and *faculty member.*

[2] Although Bowen and Schuster found that the total number of PhDs remained remarkably steady over the period 1970–80 (186), the number of doctorates in several fields declined dramatically in the decade 1975–85. Bowen and Sosa provide a thorough study of enrollments in the major fields (43–65). Language and literature statistics in the *ADFL Bulletin* indicate that between the 1976–77 and the 1983–84 academic years, the total numbers of PhDs awarded dropped 45% for French, 22% for Italian, 25% for Spanish, 43% for German, and 29% for Slavic languages (Devens and Bennett). In about the same span, English PhDs dropped 40% (Huber et al.). The main newsletter for Slavic-language teachers reported eighty-four full-time Slavic-language openings for fall of 1989 in postsecondary institutions in the United States, although only fifty language-related Slavic PhDs are awarded in this country annually. There has also been a serious decline in the numbers of graduate students in political science; Hauck reports a 35% drop in such enrollments between the 1973–74 and the 1984–85 academic years. Atkinson reports that about 25% fewer doctorates in Soviet studies were earned in the 1980s than in the 1970s (411). Accounts in the *Chronicle of Higher Education* of hiring difficulties have indicated that for a number of fields and institutions, Bowen and Schuster's predictions were conservative. Particularly troubling is the decline in numbers of minority students completing doctorates: in 1976, 4.2% of all doctorates were earned by blacks, but that proportion fell to 3.6% in 1986 (Mooney).

[3] Reskin found that for chemists "the effects of predoctoral socialization are slight and short-run" but that early publication and the organizations where they work immediately after receiving their PhDs are important (499–502). Creswell reviewed a number of research-productivity studies and found all to agree that the influence of the graduate program quickly waned and that productivity clearly reflected the employment context (35).

# CHAPTER 2

# Criteria for Junior Faculty Rewards

## Is This Going to Be on the Test?

JUNIOR FACULTY MEMBERS are neither Pavlov's dogs nor Skinner's pigeons. As McKeachie points out, academics are not entirely governed by financial and other institutional rewards, or they would not have entered higher education in the first place. But they are human, and no one who has been a department chair would claim that professors do not care about their rewards. At the very least, they see rewards as indicating the institution's actual—as opposed to its stated—value system; rewards are a measure of the institution's gratitude for recent professional contributions. For most junior faculty members, failure to meet institutional reward criteria means loss of a job. The perennial student question, Is this going to be on the test? may irritate teachers, but certainly the junior faculty member wants to know what really counts to those who determine the rewards and who are "fiddling with my life," as one assistant professor put it.

Nearly every writer on this subject emphasizes that effective development programs must be congruent with the prevailing reward criteria. The classic managerial error of rewarding A (research) while hoping for B (teaching)—or vice versa—works no better in academic bureaucracies than elsewhere. Junior faculty development programs that conflict with the incentive programs are exercises in futility.

Most departments should consider recruiting and developing new faculty members who possess a variety of interests and skills. Light suggests, "Our greatest need is to provide at least as many paths to distinction in academia as exist in the legal profession" (259). It is possible that a talented coordinator of lower-division language classes may not have to be a world-class literary scholar; similarly, a good graduate school may want to carry a few research stars who do not appeal to undergraduates. Tenuring only one type of professor may be as foolish as recruiting only quarterbacks for the football team. To use a more traditional metaphor, it is indeed strange that a profession that claims to value the diversity of humanity would want to fit all junior faculty members into the same procrustean bed.

In any case, the first step in devising a junior faculty development program is carefully to examine the institution's reward criteria. Ideally, the standards for promotion, tenure, and merit raises in each unit should embody the goals of the unit and reward those who work toward them. These criteria, at the minimum, should not penalize academics for participating in activities crucial to the unit's welfare, such as teaching and essential administrative tasks. That principle seems simple enough, but it is frequently violated in American higher education.

## The Name of the Game: Hard Covers

Around the turn of the century, research was so commonly neglected that Thorstein Veblen—who happened to be an incompetent lecturer—complained eloquently about American universities' lack of concern for it. Jencks and Riesman agree that although most colleges of that era served only the elite of America, they were fundamentally opposed to experiment or change and so appear to us "depressing and sterile places" (8). A scant two or three decades ago, serious interest and involvement in research was considered odd, if not downright harmful, to the mission of most American colleges.

Now that most high school graduates attend college, however, academics have begun to favor research and deemphasize teaching. Institutions still fervently claim that teaching is important to their mission, professors claim to enjoy teaching at least as much as research, and students pay exorbitant sums to be taught. Nevertheless, throughout the United States most larger universities—and a surprising number of small colleges—base faculty tenure, advancement, and other reward decisions almost entirely on published research, making no serious attempt to evaluate or reward teaching. One ambitious, publication-oriented dean at a sprawling eastern state university (not in our sample) is said to have condensed his entire junior faculty orientation lecture to two words: "hard covers." This caricature of the focus on publications—on, in their preferred form, hardbacks from prestigious publishing houses—is not too far from the reality facing many junior professors. The Association of American Colleges found in 1984 that an emphasis on research permeated most four-year colleges (10). For Bowen and Schuster, the publishing obsession is most evident at the research universities but is clearly present at many institutions where teaching has historically been the prime concern:

> In the groves of academe, to question the importance of research approaches heresy. Still, we cannot help but wonder whether the stampede toward scholarship—or what passes for scholarship—serves the nation's needs or the longer-run interests of those campuses which historically have been strongly committed to excellent teaching. We fear that the essential balance between teaching and scholarship has been lost. . . . (150)

Higher education's switch from an exclusive focus on teaching to an exclusive focus on research recalls Thomas More's bon mot: "It's a pretty poor doctor who can't cure one disease without giving you another" (62).

Our respondents' views of their own institutions' reward criteria are listed in table A (app. 4). Few readers will be surprised to learn that published research was seen as the primary criterion for extrinsic (tangible) rewards at most institutions. Research is clearly the most important factor in the incentive system—the consensus at all the selected institutions except the liberal arts college is strong on this point. At most universities, teaching is only considered in some minimal way; many informants said that extremely bad teaching by a junior faculty member would be noticed, and some said it would be seriously weighed either in the annual merit increases or in the tenure decision. Only a very few, however, felt that exceptional teaching would offset a mediocre publication record.

One troubling finding from our survey was that the junior professors in our sample did not think research was as important a criterion for tenure as their senior colleagues did. Since the senior faculty has more experience with this issue, we can assume that a number of junior faculty members are misinformed on a question crucial to their immediate future. At best, the supervisors of the junior faculty can be seen as remiss in their duties to communicate these criteria; at worst, they could be seen as legally liable for exploiting the ignorance of the junior professors to get more teaching and service out of them before firing them for insufficient publications.

In our study, two factors in the local reward systems were named surprisingly seldom and were perhaps underreported. First, few informants mentioned line administrators' well-known and significant advantages in salary, facilities, and power. Professors genuinely feel that spending time on administration impairs their teaching and research—the main values of the profession—and they may be reluctant to admit the benefits that administrators receive. The second surprise was that few mentioned outside offers of employment as a factor in raising salaries in their own departments, although faculty folklore rates such offers as significant. Perhaps they really do not play a large role, or perhaps professors are loath to admit the influence that market forces can exert on their departments.

Interestingly, these two factors—administration and outside offers of employment—were among the few aspects of the reward system for which men's responses differed significantly from women's. The men were slightly more apt to mention the financial benefits of line administration and the importance of outside offers. Men also claimed more frequently that quantity of publication counts for more than quality does.

## Faculty Views of Ideal Reward Criteria: More for Teaching

More interesting to consider than present reward structures is the issue of what these highly respected faculty members think *should* be rewarded. Responses of our informants to this question are in table B.

Echoing Light's 1974 findings, the overwhelming majority of our informants expressed dissatisfaction with reward structures emphasizing research as the sine qua non. Several complained about the difficulties of finding enough teachers each term to cover the lower-division classes and of getting good people to serve on vital committees. A scholar now serving as a dean shared his frustrations: "The most selfish, self-serving people are the ones we reward." He might be surprised to learn that a solid majority of those who have benefited the most from the present emphasis—the publishing scholars—also want changes. About half of the most cited scholars asked for more emphasis on teaching, and nearly a fifth felt that more careful evaluation of publication quality was in order. A number of senior professors criticized the present system's tendency to reward premature publication, trivial topics, and excessive verbiage. The Yale French professor Peter Brooks made the tongue-in-cheek suggestion that perhaps there should be an upper limit on how much each faculty member publishes each year.

No informant wanted to return to the bad old days when research and publication were not rewarded or were seen as harmful to the purposes of the university. Rather, the advocates of change frequently asked for "more balance" in reward criteria, favored higher minimum standards for teaching, or suggested greater flexibility and variety in the criteria to allow for more diversity in faculty skills and interests. An influential scholar at Stanford observed, "We're too fussed about competing with Harvard. It's a stupid thing to do and doesn't matter. It's better to have diversity, different strengths. We have a sense of community here at Stanford which is being threatened. . . ." A professor at the University of Chicago asserted, "We need to encourage researchers to put more into their teaching. This will result in better writers who write for broader audiences."

Junior faculty members are extremely interested in better rewards for teaching. A large number bemoaned the corrosive cynicism toward teaching that the present system engenders. One of the many promising young scholars who also love teaching complained, "Teaching makes no difference at _____ , and student evaluations of teaching are ignored. It develops a cynicism toward teaching." Another said, "There is something hypocritical, nearly unethical, in the implicit (and covertly explicit) advice to neglect teaching and emphasize publication. There is a serious moral issue here."

Hardly any informants complained about the long-standing academic practice of rewarding administrators with status symbols, extra pay, and power; in fact, a surprising number expressed longing for "benevolent dictators" who would reduce the time others had to spend in committee meetings. Nearly a fifth suggested that committee work and other administrative tasks not in line positions should be rewarded more, and most felt that some participation in departmental decisions is healthy. But the consensus was that the time junior professors spend in such service should be carefully restricted, because they are usually preparing a large number of new classes, because they must establish the habit of research early if they are ever to acquire it (Creswell 35–37), and because their perspective on the institutions where they work is limited.

There were a few small but interesting gender differences: women advocated multiple reward tracks and benefits for teaching somewhat more often than did men, and men were more likely to support a continued stress on research and to suggest benefits for service. Since men outnumbered women among the researchers and administrators in our study, these contrasts are not surprising.

# The Case for Research Rewards

Despite their interest in greater rewards for teaching, hardly any faculty members advocated a reward system in which research and publication played no meaningful role. Four reasons are frequently cited for making publication the main criterion on which rewards are based: publishing carries enormous prestige, it is the best indicator of the quality of a candidate's mind, it is valuable to society and students, and it is easier to measure objectively than is teaching. The first claim is true, the second and third are sometimes true, and the last is patently false. Although research hardly needs more support than it now enjoys in academia, examination of these arguments can be a healthy exercise.

First, the prestige issue. It certainly needs no reaffirmation here. All professors know that publications are the primary means by which they become known outside their universities and that such visibility can be translated into research money, mobility, and influence.

Second, our senior scholars assert that research is the best single indicator of candidates' intellectual quality—of their ability to add to the scholarly productivity and thus the professional prestige of the department during their tenured years.[1] Many of the best publishing scholars distrusted student evaluations of teaching as susceptible to shallow theatricality that soon goes stale if not backed by continued research in the field. The process of rigorous peer review for journal articles and book publication can weed out the untalented and reward the competent early in their careers. It is difficult for administrators to keep up with every field, but if peer-reviewed publishing is required of each candidate, the larger community of scholars from the relevant specialties can be involved in evaluating junior professors' competence. There are, of course, other ways, which will be discussed in chapter 3, but none is as well established or as reliable as this.

The third reason for emphasizing research and publication is their value to society and to students. The most idealistic version of this argument is that publishing is evidence (circumstantial, admittedly) that the professor is participating in "the great conversation" of humanity, the "invisible university" that every visible university must join for the good of both the school and humanity itself. The whole scholarly community must hear from the remotest members, since truth is not arrived at democratically and one dissenting voice in the desert may have all the truth; conversely, the nethermost scholars must hear from the rest of the community, since even the dissenting geniuses have to explain their truths in terms the rest understand. Universities must vigorously support the great conversation knitting the world together, because governmental and commercial organizations frequently emphasize competition and suspicion that impede learning and often lead to unraveling of the scholarly network. Echoing many of our respondents, Boyer asks, "If not within the higher learning academy, where should the bulk of basic research be conducted and rewarded?" (126).

Furthermore, linking rewards to scholarship cultivates in faculty members the habits of learning, thinking, and precise communicating, which are perhaps the main things students should learn. It is difficult to imagine students acquiring these habits from teachers who do not practice them, since important values and skills are best taught by example. As the Yale historian Edmund S. Morgan stated in our survey:

> It is a rare person who can read and think about a subject very long without exploring the edges of the discipline and writing about them. Good communicators will usually be both good teachers and good writers. After all, the basic requirement for a good teacher is to know what he's talking about. A person might have some good ideas and be a good teacher without writing for a few years, but he probably will not be fresh and interesting and a good teacher after ten years if he doesn't write.

Research is unquestionably vital to the central purposes of the university, but even the soundest idea can be overenthusiastically promoted, as Savonarola demonstrated. The enormous pressure for research has fostered bad writing, triviality, and chicanery.[2] A highly respected Yale professor complained to us, "There has been a predictable proliferation of uninteresting journals. We overreward the publishing of articles on currently fashionable subjects, rather than putting one's eggs into a more important, independent question. Quantity receives too much attention." Jencks and Riesman judge that the excessive pressure for early publication has resulted in a great many junior faculty publications in the humanities and social sciences that "tend to resemble finger exercises for the piano" (532–33). Worse yet, many academics never outgrow these early bad habits of pedantry.

Several of the informants in our study expressed concern that undergraduates were developing an increasing hostility toward faculty involvement in research.[3] Our faculty subjects thus echoed Jencks and Riesman's warning that overenthusiasm for research may result in a backlash against the excellent ideal of research and publication in the university:

> Confronted with pedantry and alienated erudition, [students] are completely turned off. All too often the job of turning them back on goes by default to critics of higher education who encourage the students to believe that all systematic and disciplined intellectual effort is a waste of time and that moral assurance will

suffice not only to establish [the students'] superiority over their elders but to solve the problems their elders have so obviously botched. (533)

Throughout this century, American educators have repeatedly implemented perfectly sound ideas in such overzealous, ham-handed ways that the ideas acquired a bad name. These ideas include progressive education, programmed learning, behavioral objectives, teaching machines, language laboratories, the audio-lingual method of language learning, teaching as the sole criterion for rewards. The list of practices in bad repute is always about one practice shorter than the list of sound ideas that generated them. Academic leaders need to reward research with more restraint, subtlety, and flexibility to preserve public support for university involvement in it. Research is too important to the university for institutions to damage the activity by irrational overemphasis.[4]

## Publication: Subjective but Handy Criterion

A fourth argument for using published research as the main criterion for faculty rewards is that writing can be more objectively measured than teaching can. That argument will not bear scrutiny. Anyone who has edited, refereed, or submitted for publication knows that evaluating text is from first to last a highly subjective business, subject to fad, whim, and old-fashioned pull. Karsten Harries of Yale told us, "We pretend that publishing rests on more objective criteria, but all too often what passes for objectivity is really its parody." He pointed out that truly original writing is frequently detested when first produced and is often rejected. Furthermore, comparing publications with other creative accomplishments is not easy, either. Aden Ross notes, "We Renaissance scholars blithely defend our publications, blithely unaware that our college must somehow compute one social work article against two paintings against perhaps three bivouacs and one and a half architecture designs" (54).

Nevertheless, the publication criterion carries an air of objectivity because the difficult, time-consuming, and highly subjective business of evaluating the candidate's writing is already done—largely by persons outside the university where the tenure decision is made—when the promotion and tenure committee holds its fateful meeting. Teaching certainly can be evaluated with a reasonable degree of fairness (means of doing this are listed in chapter 3), but the demanding and lengthy process of assessing junior faculty teaching is seldom done thoughtfully, when it is done at all, and is certainly not done by respected professionals outside the university. Hence, the promotion and tenure committee members rarely have much data about the candidate's teaching, so they shrug their shoulders about the impossibility of evaluating teaching and make snide comments about the "Mr. Chips factor" if the candidate's excellent teaching is mentioned.

# Hearing a Different Drummer: Humanities Research

Before leaving the issue of what is rewarded, we should say a word about the difference between research in the humanities and in the sciences. This distinction came up again and again as our informants discussed reward systems. The consensus was that most natural and social scientists have a view of research that does not fit the humanities well. The sciences progress primarily by each researcher's studying a very small part of the cutting edge of the discipline. This procedure assumes that the field can advance and that progress can be aided by very loosely coordinated specialists who report frequently to one another. If all goes normally, these reports are not expected to have great or lasting significance; they will soon be confirmed or superseded by other reports or perhaps even be rendered meaningless by a paradigm shift that will require totally different types of data or at least a drastically different analysis. In the humanities, the view of progress is nearly opposite.

First, the value attached to newness in the humanities is virtually the reverse of that in the sciences: a small number of old classics is more likely to be valued than recent works, which are viewed with skepticism. Humanists assume that a great length of time is frequently needed to assess the true worth of most writing and art. They try to achieve lasting value in their publications, and their most damning judgment is to call a piece "ephemeral." For the scientists, ephemerality is in a sense the norm, and pieces of lasting importance are published but rarely. Humanists regard their discipline as essentially historical; they must keep everything, as it were, on view in the same great room. A respected ethicist in our survey reported that most of his ideas come from the classics: "I seldom read contemporary authors. The great systematic authors have touched all my subjects." Scientists, however, can largely ignore the distant past and seldom need to study publications older than a decade. Hence, periodicals are far more important for scientists than for humanists. The room symbolizing the current interests of a scientific discipline can be much smaller and tidier because scientists can throw out most of the old periodicals, along with most of the books. Both these materials are lovingly collected by members of another profession, the historians of science. But these scholars are not, strictly speaking, scientists. They are humanists.

A second difference is that specialization plays a much smaller role for humanists. It is true that scientists also need their great integrators for the momentous paradigm shifts, but the average scientist can be respected for good work within very narrow parameters. All practicing humanists, however, are expected to compare and contrast widely disparate phenomena. They are expected to integrate rather than analyze; to make sense of the world; to bring to bear on any question the best thinking of several, if not all, ages and cultures; to suggest how any question relates to other questions. Robert Cohn, professor of French at Stanford, described the humanities over the ages as analogous to "a series of radio telescopes trying to pick up a glimmer of meaning."

A final and telling difference, as C. P. Snow points out, is that humanists are not confident about the concept of progress in their discipline, which is the thinking of the human race. It is hard to find scientists who disagree that their research is more advanced now than it was at almost any time past; they may only question whether the progress has resulted in a net gain for humanity. Humanists have a harder time. Is contemporary philosophy clearly better than Plato's, Lao-tzu's or Jesus's? Is today's writing more moving and meaningful than that of Homer or Shakespeare? Will any future generation ever value twentieth-century sculpture at even a fraction of the worth of classic or Renaissance sculpture? Is modern criticism more illuminating than Aristotle's?

The upshot of these contrasts is that since research and publication in the humanities differ radically from that in the sciences, humanists should be cautious about borrowing scientists' reward structures. It is probably counterproductive for humanists to follow scientists in expecting extensive, early publication from all junior faculty members. If a humanist makes any sort of real contribution, it is only after extensive thought and study. Blackburn found that scholars in the humanities normally achieve the doctorate and the ranks of associate professor and full professor five to six years later than their colleagues in the sciences do (72). The University of Chicago English professor Wayne Booth mused in his interview that expecting a great book after only six years in the profession simply "pressures young faculty to produce a lot of stuff prematurely." He asked, "What was the last really major scholarly or critical work you read by an author under forty?" Humanists should probably read a lot, publish a little, keep thinking, and spend more time writing fewer books. Extensive, early publication is not necessarily going to provide the same benefit to the humanities that it does to the sciences, and it may well be harmful.

## The Case for Teaching

A better balance between teaching and research has been vigorously advocated in a number of faculty polls and by influential national reports on higher education.[5] Boyer found "a considerable gap between the reward structures of the profession and the preferences of professors": he reports that 63% of faculty members preferred teaching to research (128). Others report even higher figures (Bowen and Schuster 19), and Light concludes that

> pervading all faculty from great universities to lesser colleges is a demand that teaching count for more. This demand can reasonably be interpreted as widespread alienation; faculty at all levels do not like to spend large amounts of time doing something for which they are not rewarded. (263)

Of course, many great scholars who were hired, tenured, and paid primarily on the quality of their scholarship are magnificent teachers. Peer pressure, a sense of moral obligation, and the sheer joy of teaching are sufficient to keep many firmly committed to excellent teaching. Of that there is no argument. Not all professors, however, are susceptible to these motivations. Some really do not like the messy business of teaching and would rather write in the quiet of their homes. Perhaps most junior faculty members would prefer to teach, but given the pressure to publish and establish national reputations for themselves within five or six years and given a finite workweek, the majority will spend a large fraction of their discretionary time on research. Junior professors are, after all, human; they understandably want to receive tenure, promotions, and raises.

For these reasons, teaching should be evaluated and rewarded. It is sheer folly to leave one of the main tasks of any institution to the idealism or, some would say, the improvidence of its employees. If we reward research while ignoring teaching, we should not be surprised when a number of professors want only to get away from the classroom to the laboratory, library, and word processor. As Thoreau puts it, "In the long run, men hit only what they aim at" (23); the same holds true for institutions.

In addition to these institutional reasons to reward teaching, there are larger, societal issues. Neglect of university teaching has serious implications in a society that may be polarizing into haves and have-nots (Thurow). How are poorly prepared college students from families with no history of postsecondary schooling ever to grasp the "rational habits," if teachers do not teach their best, retreating instead to pound on their word processors? Is this the time to further encourage the best role models and potential mentors to pull back into the stacks and never touch those who will someday replace them?

Then there may be a sexism issue—rewarding only publication appears to discriminate against women. The universities that have historically focused the most on research have the lowest percentages of women professors: at the time of our study, women made up only 4% of the full-time faculty members of both Harvard and Yale, 8% of those of Stanford, and 12% of those of the University of Chicago. The institutions in our study with a less exclusive focus on research had a much higher percentage of women professors: the University of California at Santa Cruz had 19%, the University of Illinois at Chicago had 24%, Dickinson College had 25%, and the University of Maryland at College Park had 26% (American Council on Education). Furthermore, women are underrepresented among the top-ranked scholars at most of the institutions studied. Fewer than 10% of the most frequently cited scholars at our study's institutions were female, even at the universities where women constituted nearly a fourth of the full-time faculty.[6] Women appeared to be much better represented in the ranks of excellent teachers, although this is harder to prove because valid assessments of teaching were seldom performed and their results seldom publicized. The apparent discrepancy between men's and women's publication rates may be explained in a number of ways, including old-boy editorial networks, a male-dominated manuscript selection process, culturally ingrained expectations for women, differing investments in family life, and—perhaps most important—the tradition of nurturing, which disinclines many women to neglect students in order to pursue solitary research. If men actually do have an advantage in publication, they would achieve tenure more easily than women do, since tenure decisions depend largely on publications. A study of 264 junior faculty members at the University of Wisconsin's Madison campus found that 72.5% of the men gained tenure, compared with 54.5% of the women (Rausch et al. 4). More data are needed on this subject; since women represent a fast-growing segment of the junior faculty and now receive more than a third of the PhDs awarded in the United States (Evangelauf A13), questions of gender equity in reward criteria must be taken seriously.

Teaching is especially needed in the humanities, where it is inherently more important than it is for the natural sciences and many of the arts. Like numerous other subjects, the humanities are essential to the survival of the human race; but, unlike the other subjects, the humanities are important not as a separate specialty pursued by a chosen few—the way, for instance, polymer chemistry is—but as an enlightening influence understood and appreciated by many. There is no extensive nonacademic market for many humanists or—except for historians—their scholarship. There are few private firms or government agencies ready to hire the disgruntled classics professor or to lobby for the worth of the humanities in public and private life. If the humanities are to survive and to humanize society, it will be because they are meaningful to a large number of salespeople, homemakers, executives, politicians, and scientists. To be meaningful to people who all specialize in other activities, the humanities must be well taught, especially at the beginning levels. For the good of humanity and of the humanities as a profession, it is more important that humanists teach well than that they be on the ostensible cutting edge of their disciplines. As Stanley Cavell of Harvard put it in our survey, "Good teaching is essential for philosophy as a field: no student *has* to take philosophy, unlike mathematics. Philosophy must be made attractive and accessible to each generation, or the whole tradition could be jeopardized."

## Conclusion: Professors and Unbalanced Prophets

It is interesting to note that the Indo-European root *bha* is the source of both the words *professor* and *prophet*. That bit of etymological trivia hints at the basic mission of contemporary higher education and at the need for balance between research and teaching.

First, a quick review of the role of universities in society. Until the twentieth century, religious organizations in most cultures, including the West, had a near-total monopoly on both moral authority and information. Throughout Europe and America, the churches had authority as religious centers in a religious age. The great universities of Western civilization all have their roots in seminaries that began as insignificant appendages to the churches. Now, of course, that has all changed. Even in countries like the United States that have a relatively high rate of religious activity, most churches retain only vestigial influence over a few private colleges. The colleges and universities, however, have acquired much of the influence and trappings formerly held by churches. On a superficial level, even the most secular American universities have borrowed traits from institutionalized Christianity—graduation robes based on monks' habits, titles such as *dean* (cognate with its religious cousin *deacon*), a taste for Gothic architecture and ivy-covered walls, and idealistic mottoes, often in Latin. More substantively, the universities have taken from the churches a good portion of the congregation, of the tithes and offerings, and of the prestige religion possessed as the prime source of authority and information. Universities are authorities because they are centers of information in the information age. And, like it or not, universities are among the main institutions society turns to for direction on moral issues.[7]

Toynbee emphasizes the role of a saving elite in every successful culture (217–39). He calls this group the "creative minority" and points out that its mission is twofold, entailing withdrawal and return. To study cultural problems and propose far-reaching solutions, the creative minority must withdraw from society. For the solutions to have social value, the members of this elite must be able successfully to return to their compatriots and teach the new ideas widely.

Whether they realize it or not, professors are in a sense prophets for society. Although academics would be uncomfortable in varying degrees with responsibility for society as a whole,[8] most would accept membership in the "creative minority" and agree that their duties include both withdrawal and return. The academic ideal involves both withdrawing for research and creative thinking and returning to teach—through publications and classes—what one has learned.

The relevance of this principle to junior faculty development is obvious: any program in this area must keep the twin responsibilities of withdrawal and return clearly before the young professor. Prophets who never return from the mountain to preach are as useless as those who never seek inspiration. Toynbee writes, "A transfiguration in solitude can have no purpose, except as a prelude to the return of the transfigured personality" (217). Everything about junior faculty development, including the reward criteria, should point to both research and teaching.

## NOTES

[1] This reasoning is generally accepted, and it follows logically if one subscribes to the Germanic model of specialization that divides professors into separate disciplines. Acceptance of the English model that focuses on educating elites or of the Scottish model that concentrates on training a

wide fraction of society could lead to rather different conclusions. But because the Germanic model is preeminent, the current emphasis in American institutions is on research leading to publication.

[2] Bracey, who regularly scans one hundred to two hundred journals in the social sciences and education, estimates that, on average, someone finishes writing an article every thirty seconds, twenty-four hours a day, and evidence indicates that many articles are trivial and are not widely read. He claims that "we seem to be headed toward a situation where 'knowledge production' . . . is an exercise in solipsism." Howard Christy, senior editor at Brigham Young University, comments that "the prevailing emphasis on publications—which in turn influences quantity over quality—often yields poor quality in a technical and editorial sense as well as in a topical sense. That is, all too many pieces . . . (as often as not by senior faculty) are badly flawed editorially. And the flaws are not just awkwardness and redundancy; they include quoting out of context, incomplete and flimsy documentation, manipulating sources, and overquotation up to and including plagiarism."

[3] The difficulty we encountered in contacting most of our scholars suggests that students would have a hard time finding a good number of them, and it also suggests that faculty office space is some of the least-used prime real estate in the United States.

[4] Smith's *Killing the Spirit* and Sykes's *ProfScam* are evidence of growing resentment against research. Smith's passionate history of higher education details the irrational costs of overemphasizing research and argues that good undergraduate teaching strengthens research in the long run. While much of what Sykes has to say can be dismissed as simply yellow journalism, his chapters 3 and 4, "The Flight from Teaching" and "The Crucifixion of Teaching," contain painful truths. Perhaps most difficult to refute is his exposure of the scandalous inconsistency of professors who assert that research is necessary to ensure good teaching but who insist on the right to abandon most undergraduate classes to teaching assistants lacking experience both in teaching and in research.

[5] Notable among these studies are the ones sponsored by the Association of American Colleges, the Carnegie Foundation for the Advancement of Teaching (Boyer), the National Endowment for the Humanities (Bennett), the National Institute of Education (Study Group), and the University of California (Smelser).

[6] Women represented a larger fraction of the faculty in the humanities than in the university at large, so their underrepresentation among the most cited humanist scholars is even more significant. For instance, although women constituted only 4% of the full-time faculty of Harvard, they represented 20% of the English faculty and 16% of the history faculty (Goldstein).

[7] It is also worth noting that universities stimulate economic and real-estate activity, just as cathedrals formed the nucleus for town building all over Europe in the Middle Ages. Bowen and Schuster's report that Americans see professors as having very high ethical standards suggests the moral influence of higher education (131). Despite a possible skepticism about the practical skills of academics, Americans give credence to professors' competence in their fields and to their abilities to predict trends.

[8] Many professors left the faiths of their childhoods to embrace what they were told by Max Weber was the value-free world of scholarship. Those who enjoyed success in that world were generally loath to examine the larger social implications of their work. Even the most sensitive and thoughtful of the Manhattan Project physicists who ushered in the nuclear age were slow to accept any responsibility for their discoveries. But that innocent era is past. The slowest can see that university research and teaching have profound implications for society. Professors may not rush to judgment, but few believe any longer that the search for truth can or should be value-free.

# CHAPTER 3

# Evaluation and Reward Methods

## Basic Principles for Evaluating Professors

ONCE DEPARTMENTS or other faculty groups have determined and publicized their reward criteria, the next step is to devise accurate and constructive evaluation methods. This institutional responsibility is the focus of this chapter. Chapter 4 reviews the junior faculty member's responsibility to understand the local evaluation policies and supply the evaluators with documentation of the strongest possible case for promotion and tenure.

The first principle of faculty evaluation is that the data sources should be appropriately *diverse* and *representative.*

The principle of *diversity* suggests that those evaluating a junior professor's scholarship should collect evidence from a number of sources; one or two close colleagues are, of course, not enough. Similarly, those assessing teaching should gather evaluations not only from present students but from former students and from colleagues and should use other sources such as standardized tests of student achievement. Promotion and tenure committees evaluating teaching should never be satisfied merely with in-class student evaluations or with reports from a few peers. Additional sources are suggested in chapter 6.

The principle of *representativeness* requires that enough data be collected over a broad enough period of time and in sufficiently varied situations to give a fair picture of the candidate's teaching. In judging publications, administrators should request evaluations from a reasonable range of experts, and enough writing should be examined to provide a representative—but not necessarily exhaustive—view of the candidate's publication record.

Perhaps the most important point to remember about evaluating anyone—whether a junior professor, a senior professor, or an administrator—is that the process is most valuable if oriented as much toward the *future* as toward the *past.* That is, evaluation should be done at least as much to aid a professor's future development (this is often termed "formative" evaluation) as to determine rewards for past behavior ("summative" evaluation). Albert Elsen, an art historian at Stanford, recommended when interviewed that young professors take time to daydream and to write their own "professional obituaries"—that is, summaries of what they want to be known for having done during their careers. He said, "You are going to spend forty to forty-two years teaching and researching, so you ought to create broad road maps for yourself. Where are you going? Don't spend life being reactive. Be in charge of your life. Your activities should take you somewhere."

The orientation of junior faculty reward programs and of those handling them should promote this sort of daydreaming and planning. Administrators and senior professors who want to develop their junior colleagues will act more as supportive, visionary coaches than as critics. This aim does not mean that the hard decisions of judging can be slighted, because supervisors' loyalties to the long-term welfare of the institution demand that some junior professors be rewarded more than others and that some be fired. But it does mean that both the professors and those evaluating them must see future development, rather than evaluation of past performance, as the main goal. The first reason for this developmental orientation, as explained previously, is that few institutions can depend on always having enough acceptable candidates to allow the luxury of discarding a large fraction of them. A second reason is that most professors, like other employees, will choose security—the minimum expenditure of energy—unless they feel that the rewards for extra effort are attainable and are worth the risk of striving for. The main responsibility of the supervisor therefore is to build faith—to excite and empower employees to feel able to succeed at difficult tasks that will help them and the organization achieve congruent goals. It is not enough to hold the bar high and tell professors to jump. They will simply walk away unless they see that the goal is both desirable and attainable.

This future orientation is best effected by evaluations that are *frequent, collegial,* and *explicit.*

*Frequent* evaluations are essential to help employees see their own strengths and weaknesses in time to act on the insights; good coaches constantly evaluate their charges. Professors who are only reviewed at three-year intervals usually label the experience traumatic. More frequent evaluations are less likely to arouse anxiety because candidates become familiar with them and see them as helpful. Once every year is a common schedule for formal reviews, but more frequent informal reviews are advisable for many younger faculty members.

In *collegial* evaluations, everyone—senior professors, junior professors, and administrators—is being evaluated, and everyone's opinion is considered. Professors in our study frequently stated that they would welcome colleagues to evaluate their classes if visits occurred regularly and were part of a routine practice in which all were helping one another. Junior professors will resent evaluation far less if senior professors ask them for appraisals and suggestions regularly. And it is entirely possible that senior faculty members might learn something from their juniors. In any case, administrators would profit from junior professors' assessments of the evaluation itself. Many young professors in our study had helpful suggestions for regularizing and humanizing the procedures.

*Explicit* criteria and evaluations help young faculty members see precisely where they need to improve, where they do not, and whether the criteria are reasonably attainable. As pointed out in chapter 2, a significant number of junior professors misunderstand present reward criteria, so some administrators appear to be failing in this important area. Evaluators should spell out as clearly as possible the relative weights of publication, teaching, and service activities and what are the minimum expected standards. If junior professors cannot achieve tenure without publishing an important book with an important press, that ought to be clear before candidates are offered employment. If teaching is the foremost consideration during the first two years, that should be made plain, along with the means by which the teaching will be evaluated. If service plays no role in acquiring tenure or if other broad factors, such as general collegiality, play significant roles, such information should be explicit.

Ambiguity in criteria and evaluation appears to be harmful to the whole system of incentives. Robert Boice asked a number of alienated and nonproductive professors what had contributed to their sense of disillusionment and helplessness. He reports that "the strongest replies related perceptions of reward processes as unfair and politically biased, of rewarded colleagues as more skillful at self-promotion than at teaching or research, and of administrators as vague and untrustworthy." He characterizes most faculty reward processes as not specific, objective, or public. "The usual process resembles Social Darwinism: survivors have the 'right stuff,' while failures do not." He points out that all professors deserve clear and stable indications about required minimums. Failure to provide these guidelines "gives them the single best reason for becoming inactive, isolated, and difficult" ("Coping" 6).

Explicit criteria and evaluations are also advocated by writers in the general area of career development, who tend to reflect the leading theories in business management. Glitzer and Maher state that one feature of contemporary career development is "formalized systems for identifying talent and eliciting information on individual goals: everyone knows how jobs are filled and the ground rules for getting them" (48). In their analysis, this feature gives more power to the individual employee and reduces management's control of informal, unilateral career decisions.

Another reason to be explicit is the litigiousness of the professoriat. Specialists in academic litigation fault administrators who give faculty members only a line or two of explanation about a tenure or promotion decision. These experts recommend that supervisors be trained to explain fully the reasoning behind their actions (McMillen, "Residue" 14–15).

The University of California has developed a set of detailed procedures for reviewing the progress of junior professors and for communicating what they need to do to achieve tenure. Every other year the chair reviews each junior faculty member's performance and eligibility for a promotion within rank and then communicates the results of that review in writing. The process is not always pleasant, but it lets junior professors know their prospects clearly and early. To help department chairs in such activities, leaders in the Great Lakes Colleges Association have organized a college leaders' workshop that helps administrators in conducting face-to-face performance appraisals and in giving new faculty members feedback on their performances ("Professional Development"). Although the GLCA workshop is not now a regular event, this sort of help for chairs and other academic leaders makes good sense.[1]

# Three Different Animals:
# Scholarship, Research, and Publication

The standard techniques for evaluating publication are simple and well known. Selected scholars—increasingly, from outside the university making the tenure decision—are sent a stack of the candidate's publications and asked to comment on their quality. These scholars, often with a bit of prodding, return their comments, which are inserted into the candidate's folder. The folder is sent to the promotion and tenure committee at the appropriate time for a decision. At first glance, the whole process seems standardized, fair, and objective, but several issues need more examination.

The first issue is the differences among the terms *publication, research,* and *scholarship.* While the three words are often used synonymously, they are distinct. Scholarship—broad knowledge of the field—is essential to good teaching, but a sound scholar may not be innovative or imaginative enough to be a good researcher. And, at least in the sciences, a number of excellent researchers either hate to write or do it poorly, and therefore they are worse at publication than at research. Thus academic leaders should clearly think through what they must have from each candidate. The sine qua non, scholarship, could be demonstrated in various ways, as Boyer suggests (131). Such means include textbook publication, interviews, conference participation, and essays on the state of the candidate's field. Good researchers who write badly or never get around to writing may be greatly helped by collaborating with a colleague who writes well.[2]

The second issue in evaluating publication is how much we should burden busy scholars with mounds of photocopied publications to read and evaluate. For the sake of representativeness, schools are increasingly demanding that evaluations from up to ten outside scholars must be obtained for the tenure decision (which may or may not coincide with promotion from assistant to associate professor) and sometimes up to twenty when an associate professor is eligible for promotion to full professor. Multiply by twenty the number of junior professors under review at any time, keeping in mind that the pool of authoritative scholars in each field is limited, and you have some idea of the size of the problem. Some of the best-known experts complain that they are simply deluged with mountains of such reading; one Stanford professor claims to average fifty requests for evaluations each month. Even if the material were wonderful and exciting—and it rarely is—its sheer volume makes it impossible for most busy professors to get through. Many simply skim a few things, get a superficial impression, and write the letter. A number have revolted and turn down requests unless they personally know the candidates.

To solve the predicament, several administrators, including Geoffrey Pullam, graduate dean of the University of California at Santa Cruz, have suggested that all candidates be limited in the number of pages they can submit for evaluation—to one hundred pages for example. The restriction would have the multiple effects of encouraging junior professors to do a few things well and of reducing the quantity to be copied, mailed, and read. Some faculty wags, noting that external review was once required only for the full professor level, have wondered how far it is going to go—will outside evaluation soon be needed for promotion from first to second grade? These and more serious critics suggest that local administrators and professors should know their own fields better, make more decisions on their own, and not abuse the good natures of the leading scholars.

The standards of institutions necessarily vary, and another seldom-examined issue in the evaluation of publication is the failure of most administrators to make the local standards explicit to reviewers, who then must ask for the criteria, guess at them while writing the evaluations, or write in terms so general as to be meaningless. The solution, of course, is to spell out the standards clearly to the reviewers.

Another issue is the proper values to be placed on textbooks and other published materials for teaching, on research in teaching the subject under question, on popularized surveys written for the educated laity, and productions in nonprint media. Such works are seldom given the same respect as are publications for fellow scholars, but reasons analogous to those offered in the debate between research and teaching suggest that the conventional view is not always rational or helpful, and it needs to be reexamined. Nonprint media such as computer software and video recording are becoming increasingly important both in the contemporary culture and in the academy. For many fields, some of the most significant work is or should be disseminated with post-Gutenberg technology. Popularized surveys for the educated public have a nasty habit of becoming standard works in a number of fields in the humanities. Finally, while it is true that pedagogy is often the refuge of incompetents, the president of Harvard, Derek Bok, asserts that the prejudice against pedagogy tends to keep it inferior even though the discipline is essential to the whole academic endeavor (67). The distinction between "scholarly" and "pedagogical" materials has probably been exaggerated.[3] All publishing in academic journals and books should represent scholars' attempts to teach their insights on the state of a discipline and on how the discipline's defects could be remedied. The best writing and teaching at all levels should do the same, with the lower end of the the curriculum emphasizing the state of the art and the higher end emphasizing criticism of that state. Both lower- and higher-level activities are clearly essential: to reward one and not the other endangers the entire academic enterprise. It may be true in certain fields that pedagogical materials carry adequate financial rewards of their own; if so, reasonable corrective measures can be taken in those fields. But the general prejudice against production of "mere" pedagogical materials has reached irrational and harmful proportions, and many disciplines where instructional publications result in no significant financial reward are left bereft of the best thinking on basic issues. Amelioration of this academic bigotry would be a signal accomplishment.[4]

The final issue is the prestige of the book publisher or journal. The strongest research universities may be able to continue to demand that junior professors publish with the best presses and the best refereed journals. It is impossible, however, for the average institution to make this demand for all its junior faculty members. Since there are nearly half a million professors in the United States, every professor cannot publish every year with the best publishers. Holding everyone to impossible standards will result in the withdrawal of most from the "great conversation." All should be encouraged to participate at the highest level they can, but participation at any level is usually better than retreat into total silence. Regional, local, and departmental publications and meetings are far better than nothing. The total volume of verbiage can be controlled by means like the hundred-page limit previously suggested, but most professors benefit from peer review. While we would not want to hold all young professors to exactly the same standards, all teachers must be scholars, and most scholars should publish occasionally. Students and society are not well served by dividing the faculty into a publishing oligarchy on the one hand and intellectually stunted "hewers of wood and drawers of water" on the other. Such a segregation results too often in flirtation with incomprehensible esoterica by one side and in inferior teaching by the other. The university is responsible for encouraging all to develop and nurture whatever intellect they have and to relate their experiences to their colleagues for the benefit of all.

## Terra Incognita: Evaluating Teaching

Most academics are surprised to learn that there is an extensive and sophisticated literature on the evaluation of teaching. Given the vast amount of research and writing on that subject and the relative paucity of serious writing on the evaluation of scholarly publication, it is curious that professors consider the evaluation of teaching as terra incognita. We can only touch on a few highlights from this literature, but those wishing further information might profit from Braskamp, Brandenburg, and Ory's authoritative and terse review, from which many of the following points are taken.

As mentioned earlier, the first principle of evaluation is that it should be future-oriented as much as past-oriented. It is therefore important to keep in mind that evaluations can assist faculty members in developing and can assist administrators in making personnel decisions. Some methods of evaluating teaching can serve both purposes, but many will be far more suitable for faculty development than for personnel decisions.

The second basic principle of evaluation described earlier is that data sources should be reasonably diverse, or—as Braskamp, Brandenburg, and Ory put it—evaluators should use "multiple perspectives." When administrators attempt to judge teaching, their most common error is to violate this principle, relying too heavily on student evaluations of teaching, together with chance gossip. Those who are serious about evaluating teaching will tap other data sources, such as post hoc student ratings, assessments of student achievement, student records, colleague evaluations, consultant observations, and self-evaluations, all of which are briefly discussed below, with suggestions for improving student evaluations of teaching.

Systematic *ratings by students* are used at over half the American institutions of higher education, including Harvard and Stanford. The reliability and validity of such standardized systems of evaluation are reasonably high, provided some contextual factors are held constant (Braskamp, Brandenburg, and Ory 42, 47). Many administrators are aware that students give higher ratings if they are in small or elective classes, if they expect a high grade, or if the evaluation is done before the final examination (44–45). Student surveys are more valuable if they concentrate on aspects that the students are more competent to judge: student-instructor relationships, workload, instructor's ability to communicate, course organization, and fairness of grading. Students are not usually good judges of the instructor's scholarship or of the importance of the course content.

Some faculty members scorn objective student surveys and advocate narrative appraisals. Narrative comments are probably the most helpful for developmental purposes or for illuminating reasons behind student ratings, but alone they are nearly worthless for making far-reaching personnel decisions such as whether to grant tenure. The difficult work of analyzing the comments is rarely done, and they seldom permit administrators to make any fine distinctions.

Post hoc ratings by students offer a more critical perspective on faculty members and on the whole curriculum but should only be used to provide general ratings of both. Asking alumni and graduating seniors for written, anonymous evaluations is probably the most valid and economical means of gathering these ratings. Such evaluations can also properly assess candidates' advising and other less structured teaching activities. Few alumni will have taken the classes of junior professors who are under review, but a little searching should turn up former students who can provide perspectives nearly as valuable as alumni ratings.

*Student achievement* is considered by most professors to be the most defensible measure of instructional effectiveness, but their confidence may be due to the infrequent use of this indicator and to academics' unawareness that in some subjects valid and reliable tests are difficult to devise and maintain. Appropriate national and locally developed tests are available for basic classes and in skill areas such as foreign languages, mathematics, and English composition. In more advanced classes and in conceptual areas like history and philosophy, where there is less agreement among faculty members as to what should be tested and taught, such testing would be much more difficult. However, in these areas excellent student papers and publications could be submitted as evidence of effective teaching.

If an administrator wishes to compare the test scores of students taught by two or more instructors, it is essential that the instructors know which subject or skill area will be tested and that they have roughly equal familiarity with the test. Ideally, the instructors would know nothing of the test, and all students would be pretested with a standard test at the beginning of the term to detect unusual concentrations of student ability or experience.

*Student records* are inexpensive and useful sources of data about teaching effort and quality. Information on total enrollments, credit hours, attrition, advising loads, grade distributions, and grades of students in subsequent departmental classes can all help round out the view of the candidate's teaching load and effectiveness.

*Peer evaluations* can assess not only actual classroom performances but also course objectives, readings, assignments, examinations, student performance on examinations, contributions to departmental curricula, supervision of projects, and involvement in instructional research. Junior professors are less likely than senior professors to see peer inspection as an intrusion on academic freedom, but in any case the visits will seem less threatening if made frequently. Furthermore, if everyone in the department periodically undergoes such evaluation, junior faculty members will probably not resent it at all.

Most professors will be surprised to learn that ratings by colleagues are generally unreliable, are not well related to student achievement, and are usually more generous than are student evaluations (Braskamp, Brandenburg, and Ory 66). For these reasons, peer evaluations should be used with great caution and only in conjunction with other measures.

*Consultant observations* can provide teachers with professional diagnosis and advise on improving their teaching. Such services, which often involve videotaping, are available to junior faculty members at a number of campuses but are not used for personnel decisions.

*Self-evaluations* can be extremely useful for developmental purposes but, for obvious reasons, should not be used for personnel decisions. Self-evaluations can include description and assessment of such items as courses taught, enrollments, syllabi, objectives, student achievement, student suggestions, and innovations.

*Participation in teaching seminars and conferences* provides only circumstantial evidence of teaching quality but can serve as one indication of interest in improving instruction. Seldin reports that a few British universities take such participation into consideration when making promotion decisions (88).

# Rewards versus Incentives

Rewards can serve administrators' purposes by promoting activities useful to the organization and hence are optimistically termed *incentives* in the literature, although rewards may not provide incentive to adopt desired behavior unless they are handled right. Institutions with limited resources will want to ensure that their rewards do not merely honor past actions but really supply impetus toward better performance. Most academics think that the main rewards are the tangible ones of tenure, promotion, and salary increases. These occupy the center of attention, but they are not always effective and are always in short supply. Experienced administrators know that intangible incentives are easily available and are frequently as powerful as the tangible ones (McKeachie; Kirschling).

*Encouragement* is probably the most useful intangible incentive. As pointed out previously, in the section on evaluation, the main responsibility of the supervisor is to build faith, to help employees feel empowered and able to succeed at difficult tasks that are mutually beneficial to them and the institution. This can be done by publicly and privately recognizing small achievements and then periodically taking time to ask what projects the professor has in mind. Whatever gives faculty members the feeling that they are needed and respected will pay off handsomely by instilling the courage in them to undertake worthy projects (Schuster 26).

Equally valuable is *collegiality*—the example, respect, friendship, and support of colleagues. Ideally, faculty members and administrators will collaborate to nurture a local culture supportive of scholarship and teaching—a community of scholars. When our informants were asked why they were successful, a very large fraction could point to a teacher, colleague, or supervisor who had encouraged them at a critical point, perhaps by reading a paper and then encouraging the young professor to submit it for publication or by working with the junior colleague on a class and praising good ideas and methods. Administrators and older colleagues can influence the assignment of offices, encourage appropriate senior professors to collaborate with junior colleagues on research or curriculum projects, help arrange faculty socials and colloquiums, and remind senior faculty members that collegiality is an important and immensely rewarding part of their responsibility as university citizens. If it appears to be in the best interests of all concerned to discourage certain inept or negative senior professors from infecting the junior professors with their views, the administrators can confidentially inform the best senior professors that they have been selected as role models for junior colleagues and that their mentoring activities are important to the welfare of the unit. Sometimes it is equally effective to encourage junior professors to meet to keep up on the literature, to work on projects, or simply to socialize. Junior professors are certainly not at the mercy of their colleagues in the important area of collegiality. Many of our informants recounted that their own initiatives had resulted in vital and satisfying relations with senior professors or junior faculty peers.

Another important intangible incentive for junior faculty members is their *family support*.[5] A large proportion of our married informants—male and female—listed supportive spouses as crucial to their success (table E, app. 4). A number of women, however, reported struggling particularly hard to balance their academic careers with demands of their children and husbands. Some female informants believed that men married to traditional housewives have a nearly unsurpassable advantage—cheap household labor, good food, and emotional support. While that advantage undoubtedly holds in those rare cases where a wife is willing to forgo children and to support only her husband, our male subjects generally reported that such wives are a vanishing species. Most wives have their own professions, and even the traditional homemaker wives usually want children, who in turn become another demand on the professor husbands' time. So it appears that nearly all junior faculty members with a family have powerful competitors for their time and attention.

Supervisors, colleagues, and junior professors all need to win spouses over to the sacrifices necessary to move the junior faculty member's career forward. This task is seldom easy, but certainly the professor's spouse must be seen as a very important part of the picture. If spouses are aware of the criteria for tenure and how they can help achieve it, they may be more willing to assist. Of course, some spouses will be won over if the administrator can arrange satisfying local jobs for them. Senior colleagues might consider discussing local goals and reward criteria and two-career options with spouses at a carefully planned meeting or at individual interviews. If the spouses can see that the investment needed to begin a successful career is necessarily heavier in the earlier years, they may be more willing to help make that investment possible.

For most junior professors, the single most important incentive is the tangible, extrinsic reward of *tenure*—except at places like Harvard and Yale where few young faculty members expect to obtain tenure anyway. Only 3% of our informants questioned the wisdom of the present system of granting a lifetime position after about six years of probation. In this civil-rights-conscious, litigious society, almost everyone in a large public organization— including the custodian—has de facto tenure, and the time-honored tenure-decision process at least gives the university an incentive to marshal the evidence and decide reasonably early whether a candidate should be invited to stay or leave. Understandably, the practice of tenure does not seem to be seriously in question among the group of faculty members studied.

For most of our professors, the main issue is how early or late to make the tenure decision. The American Association of University Professors recommends that the decision be made in seven years or less, but some institutions postpone it in difficult cases to nine years (three periods of three years each). The British make the tenure decision much earlier—after two or three years— and primarily on the basis of potential. Many of our junior faculty informants and a number of senior faculty members suggested that such a system should be investigated. Those wanting reforms in the present process often recommended that the initial invitation of employment be made more carefully and that the newly hired then be given more support and a greater chance at tenure. This view was often voiced when informants were discussing ideal junior faculty development programs. (See table D, lines 2e and 2i.)

Nevertheless, the whole tenure system has enormous implications for junior faculty development and deserves scrutiny. It is precisely the irrevocability of tenure that makes institutions reluctant to grant it to junior professors. Furthermore, because of tenure, colleges and universities are forced to retain thousands of older professors—regardless of their quality—thus reducing the number of slots available for junior professors. If universities had the possibility of later releasing someone who did not measure up to moderate professional standards (and it would not take a great deal of thought to work out guidelines protecting academic freedom), universities would be far more willing to hire on the basis of potential rather than of achievement and to give junior professors time to develop at a more reasonable rate. A few of our informants pointed out that tenure is not granted in private industry, at the top levels of government, or in many professions, like law, medicine, and engineering. These skeptics felt it unfair for academics to ask for the perquisites of professionalism with the job security of civil service or of union membership. Some suggested that tenure either be done away with entirely or be granted only to junior faculty members!

These considerations, along with the abolition of mandatory retirement ages for faculty members, seem to have resulted in a ground swell of opposition to tenure among academic administrators, if not among rank-and-file professors. A recent survey indicates that between 1984 and 1987, fully 93% of college-level institutions in the United States took some action that could reduce the proportion of faculty members on tenure. The number of tenured professors fired annually rose from virtually none in the 1960s and 1970s to about a dozen at the beginning of the 1990s (Painton). Professors and university leaders must think the unthinkable—reduction of tenure—and how changes in tenure policy will affect higher education, their own careers, and the junior faculty.

*Promotion* from one rank to another is the well-established, tangible reward that seems to be next most important to junior professors. Most enter the academy as instructors if they have not earned their PhDs and as assistant professors if they have, and they are often promoted to associate professor when given tenure. The most interesting variation on this theme is that a number of institutions have annual or semiannual reviews that can result in steps up within rank. Most professors like the small-step approach because it gives junior professors explicit and tangible indications of their progress and of the institution's recognition of that progress.

Even *salary increases* are not a simple issue, since professors are at least as interested in what the institution thinks of them as in the amounts of their raises; even a small raise may be very satisfying for someone who understands that it is an exceptional reward for work well done. Since the amount of discretionary money an administrator has for merit increases varies from year to year, a raise of the same percentage may have drastically different meanings in different years. This results in the familiar complaint about receiving "the smallest raise in my career after my most productive publishing year." Such complaints can be reduced by clearly labeling the best raises each year so that rewarded faculty members can see what the raises mean.

Actually, tying salaries too closely to recent measures of an individual's effectiveness may be counterproductive, if the main aim is to promote teaching innovation, publication quality, and faculty cooperation. A small college in the mid-Atlantic area ties salary increases to the previous year's publication productivity and student evaluations of teaching, among other things. A result is that one of the college's most committed and innovative teachers, who tried a new teaching technique that the students did not like, was penalized after the first year of his experiment. He calculates that the experience will end up costing him about $16,000 over his career, since each year's salary and raise become the base on which the next raise is calculated. Similarly, tying raises directly to the last year's number of publications encourages faculty members to rush into print with shorter items.

Of course, money can be used as an incentive in a number of ways other than simply increasing salary. Salary increases are always welcome, but most professors are nearly as pleased to receive research and curriculum-improvement grants, student work-study funds, and office or laboratory equipment. They see the latter as investment capital, a means to achieve their own professional goals.

Cooperation is not fostered if raises are seen as a zero-sum game where each person's raise diminishes the amount available for every other employee. Cooperation may be better encouraged by tying raises, research funds, and other rewards more to indexes of group productivity (Bogue and Brown). The state of Tennessee has experimented with awarding funds to its public universities according to their performance on several indicators of academic excellence. It is entirely possible that performance bonuses awarded to departments and units may promote cooperation and provide more long-run benefit than raises awarded directly to individuals.

One of the best uses of money is as a demonstration of faith in junior professors. Kanter found that innovative companies often "'invested' in people before they carried out their projects rather than rewarding them later for a job well done" (qtd. in Baldwin and Krotseng 13). In an academic context, such an action might mean using discretionary money to help promising junior professors with curricular or scholarly projects. An energetic junior professor at Dickinson College was astonished when the school offered a small sum to help him complete his dissertation. Since it was unexpected, he was delighted at the vote of confidence in him and now feels great loyalty and gratitude to the college.

Administrators desiring a brief review of business and academic incentive practices will find Roger G. Baldwin's *Incentives for Faculty Vitality* helpful.

## Summary

Evaluation activities should emphasize planning for future activities, along with assessing past actions. Ideal evaluations are frequent, explicit, and collegial, showing that everyone in the organization is interested in development. Data sources for evaluations ought to be diverse and representative.

Although scholarship must be required of every faculty member, it is not the same thing as research and publication. It is possible to evaluate and reward the scholarship and research of some talented individuals who publish infrequently, and it may be advisable to limit the number of published pages that junior professors may submit for the tenure review.

Teaching can be evaluated with at least as much objectivity as research is, but to do so will require data in addition to evaluations by current students. Such means include standardized-test results, peer evaluation, post hoc student evaluation, and examination of syllabi and tests.

The tangible rewards of tenure, promotion, and salary will continue to play a central role in junior faculty reward systems, but some adjustments to conventional practices may increase the effectiveness of each as an incentive. These adjustments could include hiring more carefully in order to tenure a larger fraction of the junior faculty, promoting in small steps within rank, communicating clearly the meaning of salary increases, rewarding through research grants rather than through salary increases, and rewarding groups rather than individuals for achievements.

Intangible rewards, however—such as the encouragement provided by administrators, colleagues, and family—probably represent the most powerful and effective incentives over the long run for junior as well as senior faculty effort.

## NOTES

[1] This workshop, together with the GLCA's ongoing mentoring program for junior faculty members (Wylie and Fuller), indicates a high degree of administrative commitment to junior faculty development in the association.

[2] Pulitzer Prize winner Louis Harlan, interviewed at the University of Maryland, noted an excellent example of beneficial collaboration—Gordon W. Prange, possibly one of the greatest historians of his time. Prange could not bring himself to say a project was done, and he could not leave out anything, so his books were all published posthumously by his students, who cut them down to practical size.

[3] Edmund S. Morgan, of Yale, told us that he prepares twenty pages of written notes for each lecture and that "there is one problem with that system: after a while, such a well-researched set of lectures is bound to turn into a book, and the students will not be satisfied with you just telling them what is in the book. Then you have to go out and work up some new course notes."

[4] Chickens and human beings have nearly overwhelming urges to establish pecking orders. Perhaps that can never be changed, but we can object to unfair criteria for stratification, such as race, gender, and national background. Academic specialty should be added to the taboo list. Too many academics still denigrate their colleagues in less prestigious fields—usually the service-oriented ones like education, nursing, English composition, and basic language teaching, in which women play prominent roles.

[5] The commander of the United States' North Atlantic Treaty Organization forces is reported to have emphasized the importance of winning over spouses with the slogan "We enlist soldiers but we reenlist spouses."

# CHAPTER 4

# No Publicity, No Prosperity:
# The Art of the Dossier

MANY JUNIOR PROFESSORS believe that their only problem is meeting their institutions' criteria. They hold a touching faith in their evaluation committees' omniscience and take little thought of documenting their worthiness for promotion and tenure. Of course, actually meriting promotion is the most important goal, but—as Soviet satirists Ilf and Petrov advise in their introduction to America—"no publicity, no prosperity." In other words, a dossier that does not present a junior professor's merit convincingly and clearly to the promotion and tenure committee will do little good in the committee's deliberations. Harris notes that candidates who fail to document amply their worthiness for promotion will ruefully come to understand Tolstoy's maxim "God sees the truth, but waits" (20.1).

Proper presentation of a junior professor's merit requires time, thought, and care. Candidates would be wise to begin collecting data for the review document with their colleagues soon after being hired. Among the obvious advantages of an early start on the dossier is that the junior professor formulates a clear idea of the criteria for promotion and tenure and of the data needed to attest worthiness before the committee.

Applicants themselves bear the final responsibility for documenting their merit, but the department chair or other senior colleagues should assume that most junior professors need and want help in choosing, collecting, and presenting appropriate documentation well in advance of the due date. Senior professors not only can advise on collecting and presenting evidence but can write letters of recommendation and solicit them from colleagues on and off campus. Such letters, especially in the area of university service, help develop a good case for the applicant without carrying the taint of self-promotion. Some departments appoint small committees to assist each junior professor in compiling a convincing application. An applicant who does not receive such assistance can appropriately request advice from respected colleagues.

Promotion and tenure decisions usually favor those whose dossiers are collected and organized with careful attention to the local criteria, both written and unwritten. All junior professors, from geneticists to Germanists, have at least one obligatory research topic in common: the current faculty handbook or other documents setting forth the criteria by which academic personnel decisions are made. Candidates and their mentors will want to consider the entire range of data sources suggested in chapter 3. They should meticulously organize the documents to permit easy access and to emphasize the candidate's salient achievements in the light of the current local criteria for scholarship, teaching, and service.

## Documenting Scholarship

As noted in chapter 3, in the section "Three Different Animals," scholarship and research are not the same things as publication, and they deserve to be evaluated more creatively. Publication, however, is the main focus in most tenure decisions, and the applicant's bibliography is by far the commonest documentation for this area. Of course, this list should be nicely printed on good paper and faultlessly compliant with the bibliographical style appropriate to the applicant's academic field. Most of those who review a bibliography are unlikely to be specialists in the relevant field and will need help in understanding the significance of each publication. Headings, parenthetical notes, cover letters written by the applicant or a colleague, and letters of support can explain and draw attention to significant achievements. Give the most important things first: books should usually lead the list, followed by refereed articles, chapters in books, and reviews. Manuscripts that have been accepted for publication but have not yet appeared should definitely be listed, with a clear explanation of how much work—if any—they still require from the author. Those requiring only proofreading are nearly as good as an actual publication. Manuscripts not yet accepted can also be listed but will not likely carry much weight. If any of the applicant's publications have been cited by other scholars, note that fact in parentheses following the appropriate bibliography entries and consider including copies of the pages containing the citations. Most institutions expect complete copies of all publications to accompany the bibliography.

Works in significant nonprint media, such as computer programs, text on microfiche, and audio or video recordings, are appropriate to list in the bibliography and may deserve a ranking equivalent to that of books or scholarly articles. Most evaluating committees, however, will need extensive evidence before they will grant nonprint media the weight of traditional publications.

After the publications, list papers read at scholarly conventions, noting any invited papers, which will generally be regarded a bit more highly than the ordinary variety. Papers read at international or national conventions will usually count for more than those read at regional or local meetings and may be listed first. Consult local experts for advice on whether to include copies of unpublished papers.

Candidates should also list and fully describe any other evidence of scholarly activity, such as refereeing for journals, editing, consulting, giving guest lectures, writing invited reviews, and receiving special awards.

Letters from the chair and from other colleagues inside and outside the local institution are of course among the most influential documents in a candidates' folder and deserve sufficient time and thought. Most administrators provide a modest honorarium for off-campus scholars who agree to review a candidate's publications and to write letters of recommendation. Nevertheless, many recommenders need a second or third request to produce their letters.

## Documenting Teaching

If the local institutional culture simply ignores teaching in the promotion and tenure review process, perhaps the chair can limit departmental efforts in this area to a simple note that the candidate is an adequate teacher. If, by contrast, teaching plays a role, however small, neither the applicant nor the mentors should succumb to the widespread and irresponsible academic folklore that it—unlike publication—is impossible to assess objectively. Both require collecting sufficient evidence, assessing it carefully, and presenting the assessment convincingly. The folklore has grown up largely to excuse the common failure to gather enough data. Collection and assessment of evidence about candidates' teaching deserve no less conscientious and intelligent effort than does their research.

In the section of chapter 3 entitled "Terra Incognita," several teacher-evaluation resources are listed: ratings by present and former students, measures of student achievement, student records, peer evaluations, consultant observations, self-evaluations, and evidence of participation in teaching seminars and conferences. Findings from these sources should be succinctly and clearly presented, and samples of the data should be included. Other evidence of teaching effort and talent can include mention of teaching awards won, lists of classes and numbers of students taught, copies of syllabi and examinations, descriptions of courses and programs established, and review of student-advisement activities. Mere listing of these will probably have little effect on those deciding the candidate's fate unless the listing is preceded by a readable summary of the applicant's salient achievements, such as teaching unusual numbers of students, inaugurating significant classes, and fostering demonstrable student accomplishments.

## Documenting Service

If institutional citizenship—service—plays any role in the promotion and tenure review, candidates should provide listings of departmental, college, and university committees they have served on and of other administrative responsibilities, together with succinct comments on the effort expended in these assignments. Colleagues, committee chairs, and the department chair must bear the brunt of assessing the quality of the applicant's service and general citizenship. Their reports can comment on virtues such as helpfulness to colleagues, willingness to teach difficult classes, avoidance of gossip and other disruptive behavior, and openness to suggestions for improving teaching, research, or collegiality. Applicants who find that no one is collecting such information can appropriately request letters themselves from those who know their contributions in this area. Finally, applicants could consider including a letter of their own that states support of the institution's goals, policies, and programs and that makes suitable comments about their regard for their colleagues.

## Assembling the Documentation

The junior professor who acts on the preceding recommendations will quickly assemble a sizable pile of material and, surveying it, may be gripped by a cold fear: What if the size of my dossier works against me? Good question. At the time the crucial decision is made, each tenure or promotion application will be only one in a large stack of such documents. Each application should be calculated to win approval from an unknown, callous, and lazy committee at the expense of others that may have to be disapproved. How can one be sure that the very completeness of one's application does not have a negative effect? How can one avoid burying one's merit in data?

The answer to these questions, which is known to every technical-writing teacher and successful grant applicant, can be summed up in one word: accessibility. Remember that the application will be read more like a catalog than like a novel, and make certain that those unknown, callous, and lazy curmudgeons can discover the worthy person it represents. Follow Harris's advice that "the more likely the reader is to need a piece of information, the more accessible it should be." Insert the whole stack into a high-quality ring binder. Provide a cover letter, flawlessly printed on good paper, explaining the organization of the binder and what to look for. Include a table of contents and index tabs clearly marking all main sections. Label each section and subsection of the dossier plainly. Put important conclusions first and then place low-impact supporting data toward the back of the binder in appendixes. Highlight important information with a red or yellow marker. Good taste should be observed, but, as Harris points out, "this is no time to be subtle, obscure, or self-effacing" (20.10).

## Summary

If junior professors desire promotion and tenure, they must through their dossiers convincingly argue and document their merit to the skeptical committees who pass judgment on them. Senior colleagues should assist with acquiring and providing evidence of junior professors' worth to give candidates the benefit of experienced judgment and to reduce the need for self-promotion.

A wide range of appropriate data on the candidate's scholarship, teaching, and service should be collected; too much material is better than too little. The dossier should be organized attractively to emphasize the candidate's significant achievements in the light of local criteria for promotion and tenure and to ensure reviewers easy access to the most important information. To present properly a junior professor's merit requires time, thought, and care; candidates would be wise to begin collecting data for the review document with their colleagues soon after being hired.

# CHAPTER 5

# Improving Junior Faculty Research

## Why Organize a Research-Improvement Program?

WHILE IT COULD be argued that specialized research is the one thing graduate schools consistently prepare their students to do, programs to develop junior faculty research skills further are still needed. American graduate training is an important, carefully supervised apprentice period, but the first job is usually a very different situation, where the junior faculty member struggles to prepare for several new classes, to advise and supervise, to make a home in a new geographic location, and perhaps even to complete a dissertation. A young academic leaves a routine of almost daily, structured contact with peers and teachers for a relatively lonely struggle with pressing new demands at the first job. For many, the urgent everyday tasks displace the important but less urgent responsibilities of scholarship. Professors' first employment influences their careers much more than graduate training does (Creswell 35–37), and those who fail to establish effective habits of research and writing early in their careers probably never will (40–41). A number of American academic leaders discovered this between 1975 and 1985, when they tried to pressure nonpublishing senior faculty members to begin publishing late in their careers; the most notable result of this push to research was the alienation of many nonpublishing senior professors (Bowen and Schuster 139–42). (Teaching is probably also subject to the rule that habits of excellence must be learned early if they are ever to be learned, although the evidence is less definite than it is for research.)

The second argument for establishing a research-improvement program for junior professors is that university-level research in the United States annually uses around $9.6 billion, $2.3 billion of which is provided by the universities themselves ("Campus").[1] Some fraction of those huge sums should be spent on assisting young researchers to get started right.

## Effective Design of Junior Faculty Development Programs

Before delving into the specifics of developing research expertise, we should review a few general principles. The first principle of faculty development—

and of any continuing interdisciplinary program—is to establish firm *administrative support*. Many good projects can be started from the grass roots, but the personal interest of institutional leaders is usually necessary to ensure a critical mass of participants. Such support includes a solid and well-publicized agreement on the development program's goals and on their significance for the institution. Young professors must be convinced that the program is important for them, as well as for the administration that determines their futures, or they will participate grudgingly at best. Furthermore, a good junior faculty development program requires modest funding, key faculty leaders to manage the program, and meeting and office space and staff support. It is helpful but not essential if administrators attend an occasional meeting of the junior faculty, express confidence in the aims of the project, and arrange some released time from other institutional duties for the organizers and participants.

The second principle of faculty development is *good management*. Siegel, who together with Nelsen studied a large number of faculty development projects for the Association of American Colleges, concludes, "Program management was far more important to the success of faculty development projects than was planning and preparation, since 'the road to Hell is paved with good intentions'" (137). Siegel found that effective programs had a clearly structured decision-making unit composed of professors or administrators who not only made the plans but followed through on their execution. Successful management groups were specific about their program objectives and evaluation criteria from the outset, were flexible in their approaches, and were skilled at communication (143–44).

That brings us to the next principle—*good communication*. Siegel found that successful programs let the rest of the campus know clearly and openly about the program's existence, its relation to the institutional reward structure, the terms of competition, and the successes or failures of ongoing projects. The Great Lakes Colleges Association tries to enhance dialogue by using multiple channels of communication to its faculty members: meetings, visits of officers to constituent units, and a newsletter that often contains questionnaires (Wylie and Fuller 101).

As noted in chapter 3, an orientation toward the future is vital to faculty development. Faculty members must be helped to plan specific applications of the general principles that are taught, to set clear-cut goals, and to believe that their efforts will be rewarded. Looking to the future is especially important for research, which frequently requires extensive planning to arrange schedules, funding applications, equipment, travel, and teaching replacements.

Perhaps the most important single factor in faculty development is *collegiality*, participation in a supportive community of scholars, what the historian Page Smith, surveyed at the University of California at Santa Cruz, called "the pursuit of truth in the company of friends." Writers on faculty development unanimously agree that collegiality is central to any successful development program for professors. Parker, Lingwood, and Paisley found that for the social and natural sciences, personal contacts with active researchers on and off campus appear to be more important than printed matter and other impersonal communications (Creswell 39). Boice found a high correlation between social isolation and nonpublication ("Coping" 5–6). Eble and McKeachie report that collegiality was an important factor in the Bush Foundation faculty development programs they studied: the most successful programs created situations in which faculty members felt increased support from colleagues (and administrators) for the goals of the program (217). Nelsen found that interest in group projects was high among professors at many of the twenty liberal arts colleges he visited during his survey for the Association of American Colleges (Nelsen and Siegel 146). Development of collegiality is a central goal in all the known interinstitutional programs for junior faculty development, including those conducted by the Lilly Endowment, the Central Pennsylvania Consortium, the Great Lakes Colleges Association, and the Joyce Foundation.

When we asked our informants what they believed would be an ideal program of junior faculty development, 89% gave an answer relating to collegiality (see table D, app. 4). In answer to the question "Why are you successful?" 63% cited some aspect of collegiality (see table E). The most common elaborations of this theme included mentoring, networking, and similar practices that provide a sense of support or belonging. Typical of these responses was that of a senior Harvard professor, who stated:

> Administrators and senior professors should be encouraged to circulate information to new faculty members—experienced professors are in a number of information networks that junior professors have not yet had time to join. Senior professors should take serious interest in the conditions of employment of junior professors and temporary and part-time teachers. Senior professors should be encouraged to collaborate with junior colleagues whenever possible: they should read over papers which younger professors have written, make suggestions, even help edit them.

Our respondents also felt that ideal development programs for junior faculty members should include group activities such as colloquiums, workshops, and seminars. Finally, several responses listed under "Resources" in table D fall under the rubric of collegiality—sharing the teaching load equitably, encouraging junior professors to apply for grants, and arranging for adequate equipment.

Unfortunately, our informants felt that collegiality was not well developed at their institutions (see table C): only about half said that it was formally part of present methods of junior faculty development, and only about 10% reported that mentoring, networking, or participating in the teaching or research of the senior faculty occurred. One of Stanford's energetic junior professors offered this assessment:

> Among most faculty members, warmth is often hidden because of the briefcase mentality. There's never any time to talk. It's like an ad from the *New Yorker*.

The ideal setup seems to be a townhouse in Santa Barbara, a BMW to take you to campus to dispense your wisdom and then as quickly to whisk you back home to your word processor. The new faculty are very detached and cynical. It gives me physical discomfort in the gut.

When asked whether anything or anyone had hindered their development, our informants most frequently listed lack of an encouraging or achievement-minded atmosphere as their worst problem (see table F).

Turner and Boice report similar findings from a study of a large regional university on the West Coast:

Relationships with colleagues were the most salient and pervasive source of dissatisfaction among all subsamples of new faculty. Reactions differed in tone (i.e., the inexperienced were indignant and largely convinced that it was a local problem; the experienced were more cynical than angry; the reentry were both confused and disappointed; the lecturers were convinced that it was a result of their second-class status). Few of them found the support, stimulating conversations, mentors, collaborators, and friends they had hoped for. ("Longitudinal Study" 6–7)

Clearly, collegiality is a problem for junior faculty members. The next section investigates tactics for developing collegiality, while exploring more general issues in successful junior faculty development programs.

# Tactics for Developing Junior Faculty Scholarship

*Mentoring* is one way of improving both collegiality and junior faculty research. In a landmark study of American Nobel laureates, Zuckerman found the social ties between older and younger laureates to be "enduring and consequential." She found not only that there was a significant number of familial bonds among Nobel recipients but also that "more than half of the laureates who did their prize-winning research in the United States by 1972 had worked either as students, postdoctorates, or junior collaborators under older Nobel laureates." She points out that ten laureate masters helped to produce thirty American recipients. Enrico Fermi alone worked with six subsequent American laureates. The English physicists J. J. Thomson and Ernest Rutherford taught a total of seventeen recipients (96–100).

While simple teacher-student roles may have played a part in these relationships, more complex mentoring, a socialization into new ways of thinking about their disciplines and themselves, was a significant factor in the development of these famous scientists. Zuckerman says, "One point on which the laureates are largely agreed is that the least important aspect of their apprenticeship was the acquiring of substantive knowledge from their master." Far more influential were the modes of thinking of the masters, their standards of excellence, and, most important, the self-confidence the masters instilled in their apprentices (122–33).

Our evidence indicates that such relationships are just as effective in other fields. Well over half our informants, especially the publishing scholars, felt that mentors in graduate school or later were important in their own development (see table E). The scholars mentioned mentors as significant far more frequently than did the teachers and administrators.

As mentioned in chapter 3, in the section headed "Rewards versus Incentives," administrators can facilitate mentoring. A top-echelon academic leader can ask subordinates what they are doing to encourage collegiality and mentoring; it is useful merely to raise the issue and let all the institution's leaders know that they should be exercising their imaginations on the subject. Senior faculty members and development experts can collaborate to set up formal mentoring programs. At the very least, department chairs can remind their best senior professors that collegiality is an important and satisfying responsibility of members of a scholarly community. Most will be receptive to the idea, because as adults mature, the majority develop a greater interest in what Erik Erikson calls "generativity," the helping and fostering necessary to bring along the next generation (97).

Mentoring has played a key role in a number of junior faculty development programs, including those of the Lilly Endowment, Beloit College, the Great Lakes Colleges Association, and California State University at Long Beach. The organizers of the Long Beach program believe that mandatory weekly meetings of the pairs and monthly meetings of all project participants are necessary for establishing a critical mass of collegial interaction (Boice and Turner, "FIPSE-CSULB"). They also discovered that pairings can be successful across discipline, gender, and age lines. Finally, they found that the pairs most often discussed research or publication and next most often teaching.

In the GLCA program—the only one focused exclusively on enhancing research skills—senior faculty members from the constituent colleges of the association were invited to volunteer by submitting application forms. Officials tried to match each mentor with an apprentice in the same professional field but employed at a different campus. This objective ensured that the mentors were uninfluenced by circumstances on the apprentices' campuses, such as local academic politics and professional evaluations. In addition, the outside mentors provided entry into information networks away from the apprentices' campuses ("Professional Development"). Organizers of the GLCA program say that success depended on the proximity of the campuses, on the compatibility of the participants, on their willingness to contribute time to the program, and on their desire to deepen a casual professional acquaintance into a mentoring relationship. Apparently most of the pairings were limited to one meeting or two and follow-up phone calls.

Mentoring relationships are almost never permanent, however, and considerable discomfort may develop for both participants as the apprentice matures and requires more independence (Dalton and Thompson 102–07). This tension can be minimized if the mentor foresees the need for independence as a usual result and, when appropriate, allows the relationship to move toward egalitarianism. As John S. Harris, English professor at Brigham Young University, told us, "Mentors should produce protégés, not disciples."

There are many types of mentoring relationships. They can be formal or informal. Older colleagues can work with younger ones and superiors can work with subordinates, or the pairing may be nonhierarchical. Kram and Isabella indicate that "peer relationships" may be just as useful in career development as is traditional mentoring and in many cases may be more easily available. These authors identify three key types of peer groups that tend to parallel traditional mentoring functions (119):

| TYPE | PRIMARY FUNCTION(S) |
|------|---------------------|
| Information peer | Sharing information |
| Collegial peer | Developing career strategies; providing job-related feedback |
| Special peer | Providing confirmation, emotional support, personal feedback, and friendship |

Faculty research expertise can also be facilitated by *group projects* that encourage collegiality and mentoring. Among the most common group activities under this rubric are departmental, regional, and junior faculty colloquiums and research groups. The important features of successful group projects are informal, collegial sharing of ideas, keeping up with the literature, and encouraging future work. Junior professors tend to avoid the more formal colloquiums where they are expected to present rather finished papers in competition with the senior colleagues who judge junior faculty members' suitability for tenure.

To foster peer mentoring relationships, leaders can encourage meetings where junior professors talk about the literature, work on projects, or simply socialize. Many of our informants claimed that such informal gatherings were central to their development as scholars. Some of the most successful groups were limited to junior professors, but younger professionals also found departmental colloquiums helpful if a democratic atmosphere prevailed. In neither arrangement were large sums budgeted to keep the groups going, but in some instances a little money was used for refreshments, duplication of papers, and publicity.

A number of research universities have established *research centers* for traditionally underfunded subject areas like the humanities to promote the teamwork that these disciplines, unlike the sciences, do not naturally inspire. Humanities centers provide offices and reductions in teaching loads for six to ten faculty members during a year's fellowship. The centers frequently reserve a few slots each year for junior professors and usually require monthly or weekly meetings in which the fellows share work-in-progress reports. Junior and senior faculty members who have participated in such centers usually appreciate the released time, but their highest praise is reserved for the collegiality and the exchange of ideas, which they find immensely helpful and stimulating.

*Travel money* is an obvious and important aspect of junior faculty research development because it allows junior professors to make contacts outside their institutions with other scholars in their research specialities (see table D, line 1c). Paradoxically, there appears to be a slight inverse correlation between university prestige and travel money available: the better known the university, the less money there seems to be for travel. Few junior faculty members at any of the best research institutions in our study regularly received enough funding to cover the cost of travel and lodging (to say nothing of meals) at even one national conference each year. Whatever the rationality of such a policy for well-paid senior professors at famous research centers (and even these faculty members are reported to travel to conferences infrequently, thus intellectually impoverishing the professional organizations), this stinginess with travel money has a devastating effect on the many junior professors lacking both travel funding and its substitute: personal acquaintances at other universities who could be written to or telephoned for research ideas and advice. More disturbing is the evidence that second-rate but ambitious universities are following the prestigious institutions' lead by cutting travel funds whenever possible. When selecting a position, young academics should carefully consider availability of travel funds as a critical aspect of their development.

*Time* for research is an obvious and important advantage for junior professors, as well as for senior professors. Almost half the publishing scholars in our survey mentioned an early leave as having been important to their success (see table E, line 1a), and allowing time for research is one of the most frequently recommended aids to junior faculty development. Turner and Boice report that most junior faculty members at a large state university were highly motivated to be productive scholars, but few found the time they thought necessary for their research:

> The new faculty . . . told us that they hoped to spend 50 percent of their time on their own research and scholarship, but estimated that they would actually spend about 30 percent. In fact, they spent less than 15 percent so engaged during their first year. ("Starting" 45)

The authors found that "despite a heavier teaching load and fewer support services, the scholarly productivity of lecturers equalled that of their tenure track peers" ("Longitudinal Study" 5).

Turner and Boice also report that the modal number of papers finished the first year was zero. To help junior professors use time better, Turner and Boice advocate encouraging them to write in short, regular periods:

> Nearly all new faculty subscribed to the belief that creative scholarship, especially writing, requires large blocks of uninterrupted time; they made little effort to write at regular, brief intervals. The modal habit was writing only at

home during the evenings or on weekends and vacations. This proved rarely as productive as anticipated. For example, in the spring semester of 1986, 84% of the new tenure track faculty identified specific writing projects that they planned to complete during the summer. When interviewed the following fall semester, only 19% had actually completed these writing projects, and 31% admitted to having done little or no writing at all. ("Longitudinal Study" 6)

Boice reports good success in helping senior "distressed" faculty members improve their writing output by means of a program "with priorities on brief, daily periods of undisrupted writing and on completion and submission of scholarly writing projects" ("Released Time" 323–24).

As is discussed later, most of the publishing scholars in our survey are able to use short blocks of time, and they see that ability as important to their success (see table J). A significant minority of the best authors, however, insist that a large block of time is necessary for their writing. Perhaps the correct conclusion here is that only a minority need a large block of time and that all scholars ought to do the best they can with the time at their disposal.

Three studies suggest that there is such a thing as too much time for research: Pelz and Andrews first proposed this in 1966 (55–59), Knorr and her colleagues supplied corroboration in 1979 (Creswell 37–38), and Boice in 1987 sharply criticized released time as unproductive ("Released Time"). Knorr found that scientists' productivity was highest when about one-third of their time was available for research and the remainder for teaching or administration.

In summary, we recommend that junior professors be provided reasonable amounts of time for research; however, allowing them to use more than about a third of their time for research may produce diminishing returns. If scholars can learn to use the available time in their schedules, research time need not always be in large blocks.

Nearly half our informants mentioned that *research support* was currently provided to the junior faculties of their institutions (this proportion would probably be higher in the sciences). Such funding includes summer and academic-year support; research, editing, and typing assistance; and local matching of outside grants to provide a little extra for overhead and the like. A small but vehement number of humanities professors said that they would like their campus research offices to give them more help with research proposals in their areas. Apparently, these research support personnel are more familiar with funding agencies and procedures in the social and natural sciences than in the humanities. Several of our humanist informants said that their local research offices were about as helpful as "sand in the gears."

Proper *facilities and equipment* are, of course, essential to most types of research. Scientists are so reliant on elaborate equipment that they have a hard time understanding how humanists have made do for so long with nothing more than a few great books, yellow pads, and wooden pencils. Revolutionary work will doubtless be done in the future with nothing more than these basics, but junior faculty members in every field should have ready access to computers—for word processing, if nothing else—and willing assistance from computer experts who also understand the professors' fields, since commercial software packages seldom meet all the arcane needs of academics. Computers are usually more useful if they can be linked to local and national databases. A number of other electronic media are becoming more and more valuable for research—videotapes, videodisks, and TV satellite antennae. Acquisition and retrievable storage of these important nonprint media are seldom coordinated in any rational fashion on any campus, although there is ample reason for them to be easily accessible for both research and pedagogical purposes.

Maintenance of offices, of classrooms, and of laboratories is not something most young academics would consider in choosing a first place to work, but it is becoming a sore point on some campuses. At one prestigious research university, preventive maintenance seems to have been severely constrained for several years, and even custodial work is now apparently limited to emptying wastebaskets only after they overflow. A junior faculty member at that university spent a Memorial Day weekend in the hospital after being bitten by one of the hundreds of spiders in her office; elsewhere on campus, a mouse in a departmental commons has been in residence so long that faculty members thought of nominating it for tenure. Clearly, the maintenance issue is much larger than junior faculty development and involves important, knotty issues of funding priorities, but it is a factor that junior faculty candidates should weigh along with other considerations.[2]

## The Research Process: Advice from the Experts

Academic leaders supervising junior colleagues want to help them overcome the well-known obstacles to publication: lack of ideas, lack of time, poor research strategies, writing difficulties, and lack of a publisher. A great deal is known about research productivity in the sciences, and the findings are well summarized in Creswell's pithy survey. We are not aware of any serious study of research in the humanities, however. Therefore, whenever time permitted, we asked our publishing scholars a few questions about their strategies for research and about how they overcame the hurdles to publication. Their answers are summarized in tables I through N. Although most of our informants are humanists (largely professors of English, history, or philosophy), we have compared their answers with conclusions drawn from studies of scientists, so the following material will be useful to scholars in a wide range of disciplines.

## Getting Ideas: "Scholarship Is Dialogue"

The first and most important step in good research is to find a good subject. Where do the best researchers get their ideas? Zuckerman points out that

Nobel research in most cases is collaborative rather than a product of lone work: "Almost two-thirds of the 286 laureates named between 1901 and 1972 were cited for research they did in conjunction with others" (176). Although Zuckerman complains that not enough is known about "evocative environments," she observes that accounts of great centers of creativity often "note the presence of intensive interaction and competition" (172). This parallels the findings of Parker, Lingwood, and Paisley that personal communication—like telephone conversations, visits, correspondence, and exchange of preprints and unpublished papers—was a better predictor of publication productivity than were impersonal contacts such as reading books and journals and listening to formal papers at meetings (Creswell 39). So it is clear that social interaction plays an important role in scientific research, and ideas for research appear to be stimulated by personal interaction at least as much as, if not more than, by individual reading and thinking.

Is the same true for research in the humanities? Apparently yes (see table I). Since humanists are far less apt to work in teams and far more dependent on library research, we suspected that personal communication might be less important for them. However, our informants reported that teaching and informal contacts were extremely important sources of ideas for research; these influences were mentioned about as often as was reading. Two senior Harvard professors found personal contact so important that they took time to organize new professional groups to improve the flow of ideas. A third Harvard professor, Stanley Cavell, reported the interaction of teaching to be significant in stimulating ideas: "I teach in an exploratory way, which always opens up new areas for research. Furthermore, students are always coming to me to demand some new seminar. That forces me to read and explore new areas." John M. Duffy, a historian at the University of Maryland, said that "if you know your material well, you find yourself thinking on your feet, making connections you wouldn't normally do. And the students ask stimulating questions." The University of Maryland art historian Elizabeth Johns claimed that "I can be stuck on a problem for weeks and it comes unstuck in the classroom. After a recent leave, I learned more about my own research in two weeks in the classroom than I had learned in the previous twelve months' free time."

Reading, especially in primary sources, was still vital to most of our informants for generating ideas, but they saw it as an extension of personal conversation. Martin J. Esslin, a drama critic at Stanford, put it succinctly: "Scholarship is dialogue, either personal or printed." For many of his scholarly colleagues, the main origin of ideas was in a questioning, critical approach, a private dialogue with an author. The Yale historian Edmund Morgan advises his students to "cultivate a capacity to be surprised" as they read original sources: "Ask yourself, 'Why does this surprise me?' Why does it not fit with the orthodox, conventional view you've acquired? What of your misunderstandings need to be corrected?"

A few mentioned that their ideas come from previous projects. Others reported that they keep notebooks or cards with them to record research ideas, much as artists make sketches and authors jot down plot outlines. These informants used the notes for advising graduate students as much as for their own research.

Of course, it is not enough to have a lot of ideas; researchers must be able to recognize a good project when they see one. Some of the Nobel laureates whom Zuckerman interviewed modestly disclaimed being brighter than their peers, but they did admit to being good at recognizing a good research question (127–29), and they declared that this aptitude was the most valuable thing they had learned from their mentors. A physicist whom she interviewed said:

> A great scientist is someone who is working on the right thing and the important thing. Millikan was an outstanding example of this, a man who could pick out the important things. He opened up what later turned out to be large and very important fields in physics. He had a knack for finding what was important to look into. (127)

The ability to select the right question is absolutely crucial, because, as one laureate put it, it is "just as difficult to do an unimportant experiment, sometimes more difficult, than an important one" (130). The laureates could not clearly explain how one recognizes a good problem, but the technique involves an intuitive awareness of timing, feasibility, and significance. Sufficient groundwork must have been laid, and the problem must be "ripe for solution by your own powers, large enough to engage your powers to the full, and worth the expenditure of the effort" (127).

Nor were our humanists very explicit on how they recognized worthwhile research questions, but it is clear that a number of them had developed what one called "a nose for news"—that is, a sense of what will interest publishers and readers. Many informants preferred larger, integrative questions that required interdisciplinary research or a broadening of what began as narrow graduate school expertise. A few simply followed requests from publishers to cover certain topics, but none admitted to undertaking an uninteresting study just to have a publication. In fact, a significant number mentioned that their best publications concerned subjects they were vitally interested in. One scholar claimed to work only "on things I care deeply about. A book has to be an idea bigger than you, something that wants *out*."

## Finding Time to Write: "Utilize the Interstices"

The Stanford historian Lewis W. Spitz recalled a stuffy instructor at the University of Chicago who admonished his students, "Ladies and Gentlemen! Utilize the interstices." While acknowledging that only a pedant would put it that way, Spitz felt the basic idea to be sound: the ability to use short blocks of time to write is a significant advantage. When asked "How do you plan and protect time for a research project?" two-thirds of the scholars in our study who publish prolifically claimed to use short intervals—between classes, at the start of each morning, or during less busy days of the week (see table J). Morning was a popular time to write. One scholar reported that he researches and writes each day, preparing for classes and correcting papers only in the evenings and on weekends.

Few said they were able to write for eight hours every day. A surprising number claimed to have short spans of attention and to be unable to use large blocks of time effectively. This response substantiates the findings, mentioned earlier in this chapter, that large intervals of time allotted to research can reach a point of diminishing returns. Boice significantly improved faculty output by encouraging "blocked" writers to produce two pages daily for sixteen weeks and then to set reasonable goals for editing, rewriting, and submission of manuscripts ("Reexamination").

Edmund Morgan felt that large blocks were welcome but commented that a scholar has to keep a "hand in research all the time, or there's too much floundering around when the free semester comes up." He said he can research faster than he can absorb the material: "I need time to think about it, sort it through."

More than a third of our scholars preferred large blocks of time, especially researchers like the University of Chicago historian William McNeil, whose projects usually require him to read many books and keep their contents clearly in mind for synthesis. Others sometimes need long time spans to get to an archive or to complete a project, but many of these scholars do a large fraction of their writing in shorter stints. Some of them had always kept summers free to ensure large blocks of time to start or complete projects.

Both the "short block" and the "long block" camps contained a few writers who purposely take on commitments and deadlines that force them to find the time to write. Only a small number of respondents insisted that protecting time to write comes naturally. Robert Cohn, of Stanford, said he protects time to write "the way a mamma protects her baby. You have to *want* to write, and then if you *want* to, you will."

# Researching the Literature:
# The Decline of the Note Card

One of our most astonishing findings is that 36% of our scholars claimed to take few or no notes, and nearly a third claimed to take notes but either to organize them haphazardly or not to organize them at all (see table L, lines 2 and 3). Initially, we thought that only a few scholars avoid taking notes, as William McNeil does, but we soon realized that the practice is far from uncommon. In fact, many scholars seem to take fewer notes as they gain experience and confidence. The trend away from note taking appears to be growing as photocopiers and word processors make notes less and less necessary. Certainly there is an advantage in getting as directly as possible to writing a text rather than desultorily reading and abstracting marginally relevant passages. Of course, the amount of note taking may vary with the availability of sources: if one is at a rarely accessible archive, copious note taking is essential; if all the sources will be available when one writes, notes may be less needed.

A few respondents are able to avoid notes or to make them more meaningful by writing a rough draft or by forming early a fairly clear picture of the theses and main points (see table L, line 4). Quotes and ideas can be directly fitted into such structures, and thus the time-consuming and often unfocused process of notetaking is bypassed. Researchers become authors immediately, tying their reading and note taking from the first to the substantiation or refutation of their early ideas on their subjects. Typical of this kind of researcher is the University of Illinois philosopher of science Paul Teller, who claimed to "start with an outline of the paper and fill it in." The process is greatly aided by a word processor, but we found a number who said they had been following this method for years, even before word processors were readily available. The central skill seems to be the ability to put a train of thought together in one's mind. Reyner Banham, an architectural critic at the University of California at Santa Cruz, illustrates this facility:

> I write in my mind all the time. My wife says to me on vacation, "Just enjoy yourself and stop generating copy." I write longhand notes in a notebook, and rely on my good memory to find where I wrote them. It does get a little messy sometimes, because I'll write on the back of car-rental contracts and the like.

Even among the majority who still take copious notes, the note card is surprisingly unpopular. Only 16% stated that they use cards, and a larger fraction claimed to photocopy passages or to arrange written notes in file folders or three-ring binders.

Perhaps because of the close connection between reading and writing, incredibly few use research assistants: only 16% considered them to be usually necessary (see table K). This may be partly due to a lack of resources, but it appears that scholarship in the humanities does not always call for research assistance. Here the humanities differ strikingly from the sciences, where assistants perform the less skilled tasks of collecting and recording data.

Several of our respondents begin research without a clear direction in mind but soon find a structure emerging as they go along. Many note takers said that rereading and thinking about their notes is an important part of their writing. The Dickinson historian Clarke Garrett makes notes on loose-leaf notebook paper and files them in a binder. He reported, "I keep going through my notes, marking them with a colored pencil as to subject. I can watch a ball game while I read through them . . . and sometimes an important point will leap out at me from the notes." One advantage of extensive and careful note taking is that the author can go back through the files later and mine them for data for subsequent publications, as a number of researchers acknowledge doing.

Obviously, styles of research among humanists vary as greatly as their personalities do, and no one method is right for all. Among the most organized is Elizabeth Johns, who takes voluminous notes and keeps a complete research journal on each of her projects. That approach enables her to record where she is each day, what she does, and what files she searches, thus eliminating useless duplication later. Among those who appeared the least organized is an original and frequently published West Coast historian who claimed to be very haphazard, taking notes on the back of whatever is handy, like credit-card slips: "My colleagues are appalled at my lack of system."

## Writing It Down: "Yield the Initiative to the Word"

As noted earlier, many of the best humanist scholars get an outline or a rough draft down on paper quite soon in the research process. Those who take few notes are compelled to write early before they forget what they read. The majority, however, appear to use more of an inductive approach, waiting until they have done considerable research before attempting to sort their notes into chapters or before attempting a rough draft. Herman Belz, a historian at the University of Maryland, finds "enormous creativity in the writing process. Often it's not clear exactly what I think until I have written it down."

A number carefully go through their files, organizing their notes into topics and chapters (see table M). Some underline, circle, or otherwise mark significant passages. After such thorough organization, many of these authors can write their books directly from their files. The extraordinarily prolific philosopher-historian Hayden White, of the University of California at Santa Cruz, writes longish articles around a common theme, publishing what he can, and then ties them together and produces a book out of them.

Those with a background in journalism or English claimed that their training allows them to write with little pain or stress, using short blocks of time and writing to a deadline. Writing for general, rather than specialized, readers seems helpful as well—not only do authors with this aim widen their potential audiences, but they seem less troubled by writer's block or by a crippling fear of specialized critics. Edmund Morgan reported this strategy:

> I assume that my audience is brighter than I am, but is from Mars—that is, they know absolutely nothing about my topic. You must not write for other historians—write for a broader audience, for bright people who don't know or care about your subject.

Few of our scholars have as difficult a time as did the novelist Thomas Berger, who avers:

> At the beginning of my career I prepared myself for each session of writing by whimpering all afternoon, watching television all evening, and, after throwing up

at midnight, fastening myself to the desk with shackles, to remain there till dawn.

Nevertheless, few claimed that it was easy. The Harvard art historian James Ackerman said that at first writing was quite painful for him; he would spread papers all over the room and tape pages to the walls. A Santa Cruz linguist reported that he keeps most of his research in his head, and when he is ready to write, he gets out books and creates "a terrible chaos and mess in the office" while he composes at the keyboard.

The word processor—with its ability to erase, move, copy, and store text and to check spelling—is an enormous aid to both note taking and writing. One young classicist has acquired a total of five computers. But a few of our informants saw computers as a mixed blessing. Reyner Banham reported that the capacity to rewrite has had a corrosive effect on his style: as a result he has written overweighted prose, floppy paragraphs, and, occasionally, pure nonsense.

Robert Cohn recommended an almost mystical approach: "Leave a lot of time for composing. Use your insomnia, be mobile, hang loose, let the inner computer work. As the French poet Mallarmé advised, 'Yield the initiative to the word.'" That seems as good a formula as any.

## Selecting a Publisher

Collegiality was a central theme in our scholars' comments on arranging for a publisher. When we asked what advice they would give to junior colleagues about selecting publishers, the most common reply was something like "Use your contacts, ask for assistance" (see table N). A scholar at the University of Chicago suggested, "It's best if you know someone out of your university who has published with a given publisher and can recommend you to them. Publishing doesn't happen in a vacuum—you should use your contacts." Here, obviously, is an important role senior professors can play, bringing younger colleagues to the attention of editors, scholars, and other influential people who can find appropriate publishers. Junior professors should not be bashful about asking senior colleagues for such help. Aspiring authors would be wise to write prospective publishers early in the writing process, as some editors like to make recommendations on basic approach and form.

Successful scholars saw the publication more as part of a never-ending conversation than as a finished product. Nearly as common as the advocacy of personal contacts was the advice not to be discouraged by rejections. The reasons given by a publisher for rejection may be extremely helpful in revising the manuscript. Furthermore, since no publisher covers the entire conversation of humanity, the reasons for rejection by one press may relate only tenuously to the manuscript's worthiness for the audience served by another. The consensus is clear that because publishers and their target audiences are now so specialized, it is perfectly appropriate to send letters of inquiry with an abstract or with a draft of a chapter to up to a dozen publishers at once.

Equally common was the suggestion to avoid big commercial presses and to investigate the subsidized academic (university) presses with more scholarly interests and a willingness to establish more personal relationships with authors. A minority of scholars—usually those who published for broad audiences—strongly disagreed with the recommendation to use university presses, advocating instead the larger trade-book publishers.

Many scholars repeated the well-known advice to select carefully publishers that have interests and other publications related to the subject area that your manuscript covers. Some scholars recommended that humanists should publish more journal articles and rely less on books—as scientists tend to do—since articles are read by a wider audience much faster than are books and are generally easier to get published. Seeing anything in print, even a short article, tends to build a young scholar's confidence, and a series of articles may well become the basis for a book.

A good number of scholars emphasized the importance of making and keeping long-term personal contacts with publishing houses. This aim usually involves getting to know the senior editors or acquisitions editors who decide whether to print a manuscript. It also involves being willing to participate in marketing the finished book.

More sophisticated authors advised considering distribution issues like how well the publisher would market the book and how long it would keep the book in print. Patricia Meyer Spacks, interviewed at Yale, suggested, "The most important thing is to get junior faculty into a psychological state where they realize that they have something to give. It's important for them to find a publisher who will aggressively market their books to a wide audience and keep their books in print several years." For those lucky enough to have two publishers interested, a California scholar advised, "It's a business: look at the contract carefully, change what you wish, and send it back. They will be surprised, but will often agree to more favorable conditions. They need your work to make money. I'd also deal with two or more publishers, compare their offers, play them off against each other." With a steadily dwindling number of library customers for each scholarly book, however, many university presses now print only six to eight hundred copies and retire the publication after two years. This prospect provides the author incentive to look beyond the scholarly presses to trade-book publishers, textbook companies, and those publishers like Jossey-Bass and Sage that market by mail directly to professionals in education and other fields.

## Summary

Programs to develop junior faculty research skills are needed because first employment positions affect the later careers of professors more than do the graduate schools they attended, and the habit of research and writing must be established early if it is ever to be established. Sensing their own need for early guidance, junior professors seem to be more receptive to development programs than senior professors are.

Effective programs for junior faculty development are characterized by firm administrative support, good management, good communication, an orientation toward the future, and—most important—collegiality.

The findings of our interviews support other writers' conclusions about encouraging academic research: it is not usually a mysterious, lone effort that happens spontaneously in private—rather, it is largely a product of "evocative environments" in a community of scholars.

The tools for developing junior faculty research skills include mentoring, group projects, travel money to permit interaction with the larger community of scholars, reasonable (but not excessive) amounts of time in short blocks for research, research support programs, and good facilities and equipment. Most productive scholars are able to research and write in short, regularly scheduled blocks of time.

Experienced researchers in both the sciences and the humanities agree that ideas for research projects come either from direct, personal conversation with other scholars or from the imagined dialogue that a scholar undertakes through questioning, critical reading.

While the majority of humanists still take notes, a significant minority do not. Those who dispense with notes write or mentally compose outlines or drafts early in their research; then as they read they compare each passage with the drafts, revising their ideas as they proceed. A large fraction of scholars who take notes use computers, photocopiers, or full sheets of paper instead of cards. The note takers usually read their notes over, arrange them carefully, and write directly from their files.

Successful publishing scholars advise that an inexperienced researcher use contacts to find receptive and suitable publishers, submit cover letters and abstracts or sample chapters to several publishers and regard rejection as normal, try the university presses or scholarly journals first to break into print, and carefully select publishers with interests similar to the area covered by the manuscript.

## NOTES

[1] Newman recommends that some research now conducted in government laboratories should be turned over to universities (136–38). After considerable investigation, he believes that universities make more cost-effective use of government money.

[2] Some of the best-kept facilities among the institutions in our study were at historic Dickinson, a small liberal arts college.

# CHAPTER 6

# Improving Junior Faculty Teaching

## Why Organize a Teaching-Improvement Program?

A PRIME MOTIVATION for arranging a program to develop teaching is to legitimize teaching as a respectable topic of conversation among serious academics.[1] Stephen MacDonald, organizer of several Central Pennsylvania Consortium junior faculty development efforts, pointed out to us that programs for improving teaching help break the usual taboo against discussing it:

> Talking about teaching is interpreted as indicating a lack of seriousness about research. Junior faculty instructional development workshops help remove this [stigma] and legitimize the subject of teaching. They allow junior faculty to talk about teaching without feeling silly or vulnerable. None of the people at the workshop will be judging them, so if they admit to having a problem with teaching, that will not be held against them. I've found faculty are dying to talk about teaching.

A participant in the Indiana University Lilly Endowment program agrees: "Because teaching is too often a private and lonely enterprise, it is good to have a group of [former Lilly Teaching Fellows] at an institution. . . . So often it's taboo to talk about problems in teaching, but we're breaking that silence" (qtd. in Beeman 21–22).

The second reason to establish an instructional-improvement program for junior professors is to display the institution's concern for good teaching. Universities and colleges provide faculty members with myriad legitimate excuses not to teach, so a demonstration of institutional concern for teaching is definitely in order. Two of the most widely quoted students of higher education, Eble and McKeachie, affirm that "the nature of institutional support tends to slight teaching, to divert the faculty member's already fragmented attention away from the classroom, students, and learning" (7). A University of Tennessee Lilly fellow comments, "The important thing about the Lilly Endowment program is that [it provides] . . . concrete evidence about the centrality of teaching, . . . [evidence] that teaching is important to big universities. Techniques are not the issue. Some techniques are important, of course, but a philosophy and attitude toward teaching and learning are more important" (qtd. in Beeman 13–14).

The third reason for an instructional development program is to acquaint faculty members with the literature on teaching. Stanley Michalak, of Franklin and Marshall College, who has conducted several junior faculty retreats for the Central Pennsylvania Consortium, told us:

> Most faculty haven't thought seriously about teaching. They know nothing about the literature on college teaching. Even at liberal arts schools, the thinking is all vertical—people want to model themselves after the more prestigious places, the research schools. But that brings to mind another paradox: we feel research to be fruitful and worthy of discussion in every area except education. I think every college teacher should be acquainted with Benjamin Bloom, William Perry, and the new approaches to writing like Toby Fulweiler's.

A Lilly fellow agrees:

> I got an introduction to a literature I hadn't even known existed. Most of us who are young faculty members today were brought up to look down on schools of education, or at the very least to see them as preparing teachers for elementary-secondary schools with nothing to say to those going into college teaching. Consequently, we never read about learning or teaching theories; we didn't even know such reading existed. (Qtd. in Beeman 8–9)

The final and telling argument is that many young faculty members are poorly prepared in general to teach, and they are particularly ill-prepared to teach the average undergraduate. Specialist graduate schools frequently narrow their students so that young PhDs arrive at their first positions with a poor grasp of the large issues within their subject specialities, let alone among disciplines. Few doctorate recipients have received instruction or coaching in curricular design or teaching methods, nor have they participated in serious discussions of teaching or in the production of teaching materials. Their ignorance of the most elementary concepts of instructional evaluation is abysmal. It is no wonder that faculty members usually receive their lowest student ratings during their first years of teaching (Centra 152). Turner and Boice believe that work on methods and group dynamics could pay off handsomely for many teachers having problems:

> Those new faculty who did not fare well in their teaching seemed to share a common pattern. They were highly motivated but notably insecure in their own knowledge and skills. They spent some 35 hours a week preparing their lectures (in some cases this preparation consists largely of amassing copious notes from non-assigned textbooks which are then read verbatim). And, they came across as stiff, formal, and generally uncomfortable in the classroom. Other descriptors of their teaching complete the point: humorless, lacked spontaneity, were content-driven, and fostered little student participation. They were over-prepared, but determined, by talking fast, to get it all said, to teach everything they know. And, finally, when confronted with negative student evaluations, they became angry, distraught, and confused. Their next response was to blame the students—an "ill-prepared and unmotivated lot, incapable of responding to high

academic standards." Some continue to sustain this posture, believing they will eventually obtain employment at another institution with higher quality students. Others seek help. . . . A few despair. . . . ("Longitudinal Study" 4)

# Principles for Designing Programs to Improve Junior Faculty Instruction

Several characteristics of excellent faculty development programs are listed in chapter 5: strong administrative support, well-organized management, good communication, orientation toward the future, and collegiality. All these principles apply to pedagogical development, especially administrative support: unless young professors are convinced that administrators really care enough about teaching to evaluate it and reward it when it is superior, the junior faculty will not take seriously any program to improve instruction.

No less important is collegiality. The Lilly Endowment Teaching Fellows program cites the following as its founding assumption:

> Assumption #1 is that teaching is not an arcane art in which each practitioner is an isolated, self-trained performer, but a profession in which the teacher is also a learner thanks to his or her students (clients), peers (fellow faculty), and older colleagues (tenured faculty and administrators). (Bornholdt 2)

There are several additional principles that apply specifically to efforts to improve instruction. One of the most important of these principles is that the instructional development program's *prestige* among faculty members should be enhanced as much as possible. Although most professors like teaching, under present conditions most do not value efforts towards its development nearly as much as do administrators (Nelsen, "Faculty" 147). Siegel points out that faculty members' skepticism about instructional development arises partly from defensiveness about their own teaching and partly from their doubt of the rigor of such workshops, which tend to oversell the benefits of a particular approach (133). Nelsen recommends that respected professors be carefully selected to help lead the projects.

Because of the low prestige of many colleges of education, most writers urge caution in selecting and using personnel from these schools. That advice is probably sound but should not lead to the exclusion of such professionals, many of whom make effective presentations. My personal experience in organizing professional development workshops indicates that bright and well-prepared people will usually be accepted regardless of their race, creed, sex, or college of origin.

Eble and McKeachie found instructional development programs in the Midwest funded by the Bush Foundation to be generally well accepted, and high prestige was an important advantage (216–17). The authors note that the most successful programs "did not threaten faculty or increase their insecurity, but heightened their sense of worth to the university: [the programs] did not aim at 'deadwood' or 'developing' those who had been ineffective, but rather offered opportunities for the achievers." That finding is supported by other writers and makes eminently good sense.

Prestige is also a significant factor in the success of the Lilly Endowment program, according to its organizers. All participants are selected by their own chairs and deans as being particularly promising, and this is fully communicated to the fellows. The feeling of being in a select group is enhanced by the program guidelines that keep the number of participants at each university to around six to ten each year. Claude Mathis, director of an especially successful Lilly program at Northwestern University, recalled to us:

> It was also important that the fellows were selected and sponsored by their chairs and deans, and then [the fellows] set the agenda. [There was a clear sense that the program was a privilege, not an act of charity by the participants.] We had so much fun! But you can't think that you are going to set up a silk-purse factory to remake weak teachers. We picked the best and then worked with them.

Because teaching-improvement programs often lack the prestige that is crucial to their success, attendance should not be left to volunteerism alone. Perhaps an institution can make its program more attractive by giving a few of the strongest junior professors whatever incentives are needed to ensure their attendance, and then the less attractive candidates could be invited to participate voluntarily.

The prestige of the program will also be enhanced by stressing *faculty ownership* of it, a tactic that is advised by all writers on this subject. The administration can still play a significant role in initiating the program and even managing it, but the faculty members must be sufficiently involved in its management, design, and implementation to see it as at least influenced by their thinking. In the Lilly Endowment program, junior professors choose their own curriculum development projects, and in most cases they jointly select topics for the monthly meetings of all the fellows, their mentors, and the local program organizers. The Central Pennsylvania Consortium's junior faculty weekend workshop, with the preset topic of critical thinking, would seem to preclude such involvement, but its organizers, Stephen C. MacDonald and Stanley Michalak, believe the sense of faculty ownership to be crucial. Michalak told us, "The whole approach is nonprescriptive. We ask them what they are doing and what they want to do. We're not going to tell them how to teach, but we want them to reflect on what they are doing." MacDonald and Michalak are careful to involve large numbers of local faculty members in each workshop and to make sure that the outside experts will be accepted by the participants. MacDonald commented:

> Presenters should seem like faculty, not slick. Faculty are touchy and prefer to be addressed by people who look and talk and think like they do. A variety of performers is important, so that one person's personality and idiosyncrasies do not wear too thin. Use local faculty as much as possible, and in as wide a variety

of disciplines as possible. Credibility often depends on having someone from a closely related discipline affirming whatever principles or tactics are being taught. Participants must see it all as a conversation among equals, with some having a little more experience than others.

A former director of the Lilly Endowment Teaching Fellows program agreed that choice of the leaders of such a program is critical:

> You need a strong leadership from a senior person who knows the problems and can bring the group together, get the conversation going. The senior people must be known to be interested, lively teachers. If you want a good support group, the director must have a philosophical interest in teaching. In temperament he or she must not be pretentious—junior professors won't accept a university administrator type. The director must be personable, informal, lively, with a wide-ranging capacity to be interested in a broad range of issues, to see implications for teaching in a variety of subjects.

The principle of faculty ownership is a corollary of the general principle of collegiality as the central goal and most powerful tool in improving faculty professionalism.[2]

Selection of a central subject or type of activity for the program is apparently critical. There is excellent agreement that faculty members usually prefer *intellectually challenging topics* that are not limited to prescriptions of method divorced from content. The Central Pennsylvania Consortium directors say that junior professors find the topic of critical thinking to be infinitely challenging and rich (Michalak). Stephen MacDonald reported to us:

> We focus on some larger issue—in our case higher-order reasoning—and let the discussion flow from that. It works well for junior faculty, at least. We can usually expect a good healthy argument between two groups: the natural scientists and the linguists arguing for content and coverage, while the social scientists and the humanists defend higher-order reasoning.

Eble and McKeachie found participants in the Bush Foundation study to be most receptive to programs that focused on student achievement (216–17). Well-accepted topics include teaching writing, using the computer, student learning styles, and teaching by discussion. Siegel reports similar findings from the Association of American Colleges study (133). Other potentially attractive topics (inferred from a study of Canadian faculty members) might include group work, organizing teaching resources, and evaluating student performance (Foster and Nelson 121).

Closely related to the principle of challenging participants intellectually is the idea that instructional development programs are enhanced by *the transcending of disciplines.* In practice, this means selecting faculty members from a variety of disciplines and pursuing topics with broad appeal. Participants then become acquainted with the whole university and develop both institutional loyalty and a sense of membership in a community of scholars. It is not difficult to find interdisciplinary topics that are intellectually challenging and interesting, and—most important for instructional development—transcending disciplines can help participants focus on more powerful general teaching principles rather than on subject-specific issues. Although interdisciplinary work was specifically mentioned by our faculty informants rather infrequently (see table D, line 3e, app. 4), nearly all the directors of programs for developing junior faculty teaching said that it was important to the success of their efforts. My own work in arranging general-education faculty seminars and workshops firmly supports their views: professors enjoy the chance to escape their professional boxes and to discuss larger issues.

# Specific Tactics for Improving Junior Faculty Teaching

*Mentoring* is as powerful an influence on junior faculty teaching as it is on research. A number of mentoring strategies and tactics are listed in chapter 3, in the section "Rewards versus Incentives," and others are discussed in chapter 5, under "Tactics for Developing Junior Faculty Scholarship." In these methods, senior administrators ask subordinates what is being done to encourage collegiality and mentoring, department chairs remind their senior faculty members that collegiality is an important responsibility of members of a community of scholars, and leaders encourage peer relationships within and across departmental lines. Mentoring pairs should meet frequently and regularly.

Academic leaders can do several things to foster mentoring relationships that improve teaching. The simplest tactic is for department leaders to encourage junior professors teaching a course for the first time to approach experienced colleagues for syllabi, reading lists, and other course materials. Most senior professors are flattered that their ideas are considered by both the chair and the new faculty member to be worth studying. While such informal sharing implies no long-term commitment, it can initiate a lasting professional bond. One way to start a trial relationship that may bloom into a full-grown mentoring commitment is simply to assign junior professors to teach with senior professors in core courses. Those at the University of Chicago who have participated in team-taught undergraduate core courses with eminent senior colleagues claim that the experience was one of the most stimulating and influential of their entire careers. Another method to arrange mentoring is used at Beloit College and is funded by the Joyce Foundation: carefully selected retiring faculty members are engaged to remain a year or more at part salary to work closely with their replacements, who carry a reduced teaching load but receive a full salary. The Joyce Fellows all meet in one group monthly, and participant acceptance of the program appears to be high. Some of the program's popularity may be due to the released time the junior professors receive, but the program deserves further study and adaptation elsewhere. In a technique tried at Furman University, experienced and inexperienced teachers (often from separate disciplines) were given one course of released time and paired to work together to improve each other's teaching. Their activities included extensive intervisitation; discussions of syllabi, assignments, tests, papers, and ways to improve classes; video recording of classes and subsequent discussion of the recordings (Hipps 44–45). Most of the Lilly Endowment Teaching Fellows programs use another technique: supervisors select a few fellows (from six to nine) and, in consultation with the fellows, choose a mentor for each. The fellows and their mentors work together on a course-improvement project all year, with or without released time.

In fact, *curriculum development projects* are widely and successfully used to improve junior faculty teaching, although they do not necessarily involve mentoring. Since, typically, new faculty members are pressed for time to develop their courses and have at least as great a teaching and publishing load as they will ever have, providing them with resources and time to work up new courses or new approaches to old courses frequently pays off directly and immediately in better instruction and in increased emotional involvement of the professors with their courses. Perhaps most important, funds and encouragement to work on curriculum development indicate to the young professor that excellent preparation for teaching is important to the institution. We should note here Eble and McKeachie's recommendation that curriculum development programs focus on the basics of teaching rather than on materials development or on radical new methods. They call for instructional development projects that help young faculty members in "developing basic skills in test construction, conducting discussion, lecturing, and providing feedback to students through comments on papers" (222).

Summer support money and released time are two options for buying professorial time, and modest funding for reference books, equipment, audiovisual aids, and printed course materials is essential. The thrifty administrator may hesitate to put much money into a course that the junior faculty member may not be teaching in a few years, given that the young professor's position is temporary and that most teaching assignments are rotated. These considerations argue for pairing another faculty member—especially a senior one—with the prime recipient, since the second team member would then share in the thinking that motivates the course and materials, would double the possibility that the materials will be used, and would represent another voice advocating the new approach before the academic unit. Of course, it is vital that all team members be compatible.

Research is usually expected to result in publication, while instruction is not. Participants in a curriculum development project, however, should consider publishing some aspect of the course materials—collections of readings, audiovisuals, lecture notes, exercises, computer programs, or an article about the whole approach. Robert M. Diamond, of Syracuse University, told us his impression that assigning a competent professional from the university's design and evaluation office to each Lilly Endowment team significantly raised the quality of many projects and helped result in a number of publications. Thomas M. Schwen and Mary Deane Sorcinelli, faculty development leaders at

Indiana University, also feel that professionals from various faculty support offices were important to their junior faculty development efforts (91).

*Group activities* are as commonly suggested for fostering teacher development as they are for developing research expertise. Such practices to promote teaching usually aid collegiality and can easily be made interdisciplinary. They may take the forms of afternoon or Saturday workshops, weekend retreats, week-long classes, weekly luncheons, or term-length classes, and they may be mixed with other activities. The Lilly Endowment combines its project-oriented mentoring activities with monthly meetings of the fellows and their mentors, together with two national conferences during the year. Comments of the Lilly fellows indicate that the group activities were central to the success of the program. Similarly, Boice and Turner believe that their monthly group meetings of all mentoring pairs were vital for their project ("FIPSE-CSULB"). The Central Pennsylvania Consortium uses a single weekend retreat with a combination of plenary sessions and discipline groups in which local workshop alumni lead discussions. Time to socialize during the workshop and time later for group follow-up sessions are both important to the consortium's program. William J. Hynes, director of the faculty development program of Regis College, recommends tying competitive curriculum grants to a mandatory short course on teaching (33). Faculty members receiving summer grants to redesign courses can be required to attend a one-week workshop on improving instructional techniques.

In Great Britain, intensive courses on university teaching are offered to newcomers to the teaching staff at almost every university (Seldin 26). Roughly 70% of the new teachers attend these courses, which usually last three or four days and take place just before fall sessions begin. The courses generally focus on lecturing and on teaching aids. Each September the respected Institute of Educational Technology of the University of Surrey offers an intensive seven-day course, whose instructor—L. R. B. Elton—aims to get "professors to bring to their teaching the same critical, doubting, and creative attitudes they bring habitually to their research activities" (42).

Although there is clearly a need for an initial orientation session for new faculty members, most directors of junior faculty programs recommend *avoiding the first year* when scheduling serious teaching development programs. The rationale given is that new professors need the first year of experience to focus their thinking and to acquire concrete examples of the general principles to be discussed. Furthermore, new faculty members are so harried with organizing their basic course materials and getting acquainted with procedures, equipment, colleagues, and buildings that they are not generally receptive to extended philosophical discussions on the larger aims of the curriculum.

*Teaching resource centers* have been established at a number of leading universities to advocate and assist teaching improvement (Alfonsi). One of the oldest continuously functioning centers was established in 1961 at the University of Michigan. In the mid-1970s the Danforth Foundation invested $2.3 million to establish teaching centers at five universities, of which only

Harvard, Northwestern, and Stanford still maintained them a decade later, with other funding. In 1983 Carnegie Mellon University established a center that collects video recordings of excellent teachers, issues handbooks for inexperienced teachers, and conducts teaching workshops, among other things.

These centers apparently can play an important role in improving junior faculty teaching. Unfortunately, too many faculty members see them as purely remedial agencies to help those with specific teaching problems, although a number of professors mentioned that they had benefited from video recordings of their classroom performances, especially when staffers from the center viewed the recordings with them. Perhaps the most important value of these centers is that they serve as official campus advocates for good teaching and often provide leadership for teaching improvement programs, including those for junior faculty members.

*Intervisitation*, the mutual visiting of classes by colleagues, can be a powerful tactic for improving teaching, especially if the emphasis is on development rather than evaluation. As explained in chapter 3, visiting should be done frequently, rather casually, and with good communication beforehand in arranging the visits and afterwards in sharing impressions. Some senior faculty members among our informants fondly remembered the helpful effects of such intervisitation in bygone years at teaching-oriented liberal arts colleges (frequently women's institutions) where it was common.

*Student advice* is important for improving teaching and is probably most valuable if sought in essay or narrative form early in the term, when there is still time to make changes. Teachers in large classes might select a small group of conscientious, good-to-excellent students to represent the rest. This group can be requested to make suggestions, to meet periodically with the teacher, and perhaps to help with minor class-management chores. Students usually appreciate the opportunity to work closely with a teacher, and teachers usually report that such small groups can be very helpful. An interesting variation on this theme is offered at Dickinson College: teachers can apply to the administration for an experienced student observer who will receive the minimum wage to sit toward the back of the class throughout the course and to make suggestions privately to the teacher.

# Some Programs for Improving Junior Faculty Teaching

The Lilly Endowment has sponsored well over thirty junior faculty instructional development programs in large public universities east of the Mississippi River and has developed a set of guidelines for the programs (Beeman). Leaders at each selected institution carefully choose six to ten promising junior professors and assign them mentors. All participants receive a slight reduction in teaching load to work in pairs on curriculum development projects for a year; the whole group meets at the beginning of the year and then again each month or so to share experiences and discuss teaching and other professional questions. Each Lilly Fellow attends two national conferences on college teaching during the fellowship year and thus has the opportunity to compare notes with junior professors at other institutions. A number of universities, including Northwestern University, the University of Wisconsin system, and Indiana University, have continued some form of the program under their own funding after the end of the Lilly grant period. The Lilly format ensures that participants feel honored to have been selected and therefore endows the program and the practice of teaching with prestige.

The *Central Pennsylvania Consortium* has long sponsored junior faculty development programs, of which the most successful is a weekend retreat centering on development of critical thinking across the curriculum (Michalak). The retreat, always located in a beautiful setting, consists of plenary sessions alternating with small-group discussions. The members of each small group belong to the same discipline, including the group leader, who is invariably a past workshop participant. All new faculty members are invited; attendance is urged but not required. Administrators are excluded from the retreat so that there will be no taint of evaluation in what is supposed to be a purely developmental activity. The organizers of the consortium's retreats feel that the pleasant setting, the two-day format, and the intellectually challenging theme are all significant in the success of their program.

The directors of both the Lilly Endowment and the Central Pennsylvania Consortium stress the importance of involving local faculty members rather than relying solely on outside experts; both use lectures alternating with carefully structured active contributions by all participants; both wait until the new professors have two semesters of teaching experience before beginning the programs; both emphasize the value of dedicating large blocks of time for faculty socializing.

The *Joyce Foundation,* as mentioned previously in this chapter, in the section "Specific Tactics for Improving Junior Faculty Teaching," has funded a mentoring program for junior professors at Beloit College. Selected retiring professors remain at the college working part-time as mentors with the junior professors who replace them. All mentors and their partners meet in one group monthly.

The *California State University at Long Beach,* together with the Fund for the Improvement of Postsecondary Education, funded an ambitious mentoring project for junior faculty members, mentioned in chapter 5, under the heading "Tactics for Developing Junior Faculty Scholarship." The directors of the program assigned senior professors to junior colleagues (often in different disciplines), paid the senior professors a stipend for participation, and visited them in their offices to ensure that they were meeting weekly with their protégés. All project participants met monthly to share their experiences (Boice and Turner, "FIPSE-CSULB").[3]

The Division of Instructional Development of the *University of Illinois* has organized ninety-minute seminars for new faculty members in each college and in various departments. The division has been successful at enlisting departments and colleges to take the initiative in organizing these seminars, which have focused on instructional issues such as cognitive styles, course management, cheating, and alternatives to the lecture.

The *University of Oklahoma* in the fall of 1988 began a semester-long program under Dee Fink's direction for new faculty members of all ranks. Each week new professors meet on a voluntary basis for a free lunch followed by a ninety-minute program focusing primarily on teaching and general orientation; a few sessions are devoted to research. Each session is offered on Monday and repeated on Thursday to minimize time conflicts and to keep group size manageable. Seventy percent of the new faculty members attend these sessions regularly (Fink, "Seminar").

The *University of Texas at Austin* holds a teaching seminar for all new professors during the three days preceding fall registration. The seminar features plenary sessions followed by meetings in which participants choose one of three topics. Attendance at the seminar averages from 30% to 50% of the newly hired professors, perhaps because the seminar is scheduled at a very difficult time for most.

*British universities* have long provided development programs for junior faculty members. Since the mid-1970s all universities in Great Britain have offered "new staff an introduction to university organization and services either separately or as part of an introductory training course" (Seldin 26–27). The orientation program usually takes about a day and often includes socializing with university officials. Furthermore, all but four of the forty-six British universities offer a course for newcomers to the teaching staff. Such courses are made up largely of lectures, are attended by about 70% of those eligible, and typically are squeezed into three or four days before the fall term begins. Most of the courses focus on improving lectures and teaching aids, although a few cover such topics as small-group instruction, project teaching, and assessment of students.

(For the addresses and telephone numbers of these programs, see appendix 2.)

# What Is Good Teaching? Apollo and Dionysus

We did not ask our informants what good scholarship is, because we sensed that most institutions are more concerned with the process for identifying quality than with the definition of it. Institutions can probably pursue a similar strategy for avoiding a precise definition of good teaching, establishing instead a process for evaluating teaching. However, since some of our publishing scholars claimed that good teaching is difficult to define, we decided to see whether the better teachers among our informants shared any common definition of good teaching. We therefore began asking them, "What is good teaching? How do you know it when you see it or have done it?"

The answers, summarized in table O, indicate a surprising agreement that good teaching is characterized primarily by its effect on students, by what a number of writers call *outcomes*. Good teaching, according to 51% of those asked, is marked by a high degree of student interest or participation, and the more mature teachers mentioned this much oftener than did junior faculty members. Mary Carruthers, director of graduate studies and professor of English at the University of Illinois at Chicago, typifies this group: "I know I've done well when the class gets that 'Aha!' look—in other words, when they're interested and involved. The teacher is a facilitator between the student and the material. We're not paid to be just showmen." The Yale classicist Donald Kagan advised:

> In the information age there are plenty of ways to get information across to students, so the lecture shouldn't mainly focus on that goal.[4] I prefer topical approaches and the use of central questions. We should not make the subject a mystery but should give the student the feeling that anyone can learn the basics and join in the conversation. I like to give the feeling, "Come with me and let's see what's here."

Kagan implies that the most important element in good teaching is involving students to enable them to think and learn on their own. Of our informants, 46% specifically defined good teaching as helping students acquire this independent style of inquiry. This group is typified by a Shakespeare scholar at the University of California at Santa Cruz, Michael Warren, who described good teaching as "an act of liberation for the students, a process of giving them the tools to go on themselves from where you leave off. Good teaching is enabling. I try to show how I come to a conclusion, not just the conclusion itself."

A smaller number mentioned what writers in this area often call *inputs*, such as instructor enthusiasm, clear presentation of content, interest in students, and good organization.

The importance of enthusiasm was stressed by 23% of our respondents, a concern that is closely related to that of conveying the significance of the subject (stressed by 14%). As a University of Illinois historian said, "Good teaching conveys an enthusiasm and love for the subject which you have yourself. Information is not the important thing—I want to convey the wonder, the beauty, the glory of history." Vincent Scully, an art historian at Yale, agreed and suggested that engaging lectures develop in two distinct stages:

> Teaching is a combination of Apollo and Dionysus. When you plan, it must be very intellectual, Apollonian, thorough, logical. I only teach things I know very well. The challenge is to balance clarity with the complexity of reality. The aesthetic reaction is constantly leaping out of the logical boxes you set for yourself. Then when you deliver the lecture, you must hope that the emotional, intuitive, Dionysian elements take over and the lecture takes on a rhythm of its own.

Clear presentation of content was mentioned by 20% of our informants, and 11% noted good organization. This aspect was exemplified in the response of the Stanford art historian Albert Elsen: "Keep it simple. Ask yourself to state in one sentence what a thinking person should know about this lecture topic." The University of Maryland historian Allison G. Olson advised, "The cardinal rule is that you must be organized. And it is impossible to be too simple and clear. Outlining is very helpful to narrow the range of topics and points you try to cover in a lecture."

As mentioned in the first section of this chapter, Turner and Boice found that ineffective new college teachers have poor rapport with their students; these instructors tend to be insecure and to concentrate compulsively on their subject matter to the detriment of relations with their students and of students' involvement in the classwork ("Starting"). Classroom rapport was uppermost for 14% of our informants, however. Philip Lockhart, a classicist at Dickinson College, saw good relations with students as essential to excellence: "Before you teach, you must love both your discipline and your students. After you teach, they should love both the discipline and you. If you just love the students and not your discipline, you will only be sentimental and ineffectual. If you love your discipline but not the students, you'll simply be a pedant." The collegiality that is desirable between senior and junior faculty members is equally beneficial between teachers and students: the best professors are those who really care that their students grow, succeed, and feel valued as human beings and not only as fellow scholars.

Perhaps our most memorable interview was with the controversial University of California at Santa Cruz professor emeritus of history Page Smith— Harvard-educated, a former dean, and a great bear of a man who cares passionately about students and teaching. Smith's prescription for good teaching was simple: "Just love the students." When met with a quizzical look and asked if methods meant nothing, Smith explained that he shared Woodrow Wilson's suspicion of pedagogy as a formalized barrier between teacher and students,[5] and he said, "Only if you care for students and they know it can you demand their best from them." Without this concern, he said, students are seldom motivated to do their best, and any criticism is corrosive and debilitating. In a provocative essay entitled "The Inhuman Humanities," Smith writes the following about students:

> If we do not love and care for them, if we do not place them in the center of our thinking and doing, if we persist in thinking that they are merely incidental to or distracting from our serious scholarly concerns, then there is, quite literally, no hope for higher education. (*Dissenting Opinions* 123)

Keeping in mind Smith's warning about the dehumanizing dangers of a narrow focus on cold method, we conclude from our respondents' comments that both teacher inputs and learner outcomes are important factors in improving teaching. The best teachers all focus on the students and adroitly vary their methods to raise student interest and achieve broader learning. And, like Page Smith, they show their concern for their students.

Our results agree generally with the recommendations of writers on college-level teaching. Eble and McKeachie (216–17), Nelsen ("Faculty" 148), and others concur with the obvious but sometimes overlooked view that improving student learning should be a main goal of faculty instructional development programs. Braskamp, Brandenburg, and Ory agree that no single instructional strategy is always superior and that good teachers must continually assess not only methods but also student learning and input factors such as student educational background and class size.

Surveying the literature on teaching effectiveness, Donald reports progress toward understanding student learning, but considerable research is needed to clarify the aims and valid measures of learning. Reviewing studies of teaching inputs, she reveals that *students* in all fields believed mastery of the subject, orderliness of presentation, and encouragement of class participation to be characteristic of excellent teachers. Students in the sciences stressed course organization somewhat more than did those in the humanities, who in turn emphasized enthusiasm and a sense of humor (10). She reports a study that, unsurprisingly, found student learning to be highest in courses that students value highly (13). That finding could suggest that instructors who are able to convey enthusiasm for a course might well be serving student learning.

The material in this section holds several implications for improving the teaching of young faculty members. The sheer quantity of facts a teacher presents is not as important to good teaching as a number of other factors, which junior professors should be helped to understand:

- Most young teachers need to *care more about the students*— about how the students are being involved and how well they are grasping what is taught.
- *Orderliness and clarity* are more important to good teaching than is the number of facts presented.
- It is important to *ponder the aims* of one's teaching: for many courses, an appropriate goal may be to help students acquire a new mode of thinking.
- *Enthusiasm and humor* are widely appreciated by students and play an important role in improving class rapport.

## Summary

Programs for improving junior faculty teaching are needed because many young professors are poorly prepared to teach. Furthermore, such programs legitimize teaching as a topic of campus conversation, demonstrate institutional support for better teaching, and acquaint faculty members with the literature on teaching.

The general factors important in faculty development programs include collegiality, administrative support, good management, good communication, and an orientation toward the future. All these considerations, especially collegiality and administrative support, apply to programs for improving junior faculty teaching. Teaching development programs also require prestige, faculty ownership, intellectual challenge, and the transcending of disciplines.

The specific means for improving junior faculty teaching include mentoring, curriculum development projects, faculty group projects (classes, workshops, retreats), teaching consultants, resource centers, intervisitation, and advice from students. Many experts recommend scheduling such programs only after the first year of teaching.

Junior professors should be helped to realize that the quantity of facts conveyed is not the only factor in good teaching. Among other elements are orderliness, clarity, humor, enthusiasm, the ability to stimulate student involvement and new modes of thinking, and genuine concern for students.

These points are drawn from our survey, from the literature, and from junior faculty development programs sponsored by the Central Pennsylvania Consortium, the Lilly Endowment, Beloit College, California State University at Long Beach, the University of Illinois at Urbana, the University of Oklahoma, the University of Texas at Austin, and universities in Great Britain.

## NOTES

[1] The arguments for placing more emphasis on evaluating and rewarding teaching are presented in chapters 2 and 3, so we will not cover that ground again here except to stress that these two steps must be first in any program to improve instruction by junior faculty members.

[2] One of the first administrators to learn the lesson of faculty ownership was Robert of Courson, a papal legate in twelfth- and thirteenth-century France. His attempts to institute reforms throughout France were singularly unsuccessful as long as he used high-handed methods, but he achieved enduring success when he changed to a more democratic management style to bring order from the chaos reigning in the competing schools of Paris. He worked "closely with the masters and scholars to reform the schools" that would soon thereafter become the University of Paris (Ferruolo 305).

[3] The junior faculty mentoring program at California State University at Long Beach was directed by Robert Boice and Jim Turner. Boice has since moved to the State University of New York at Stony Brook and Turner to the University of California at Los Angeles.

[4] The architectural critic Reyner Banham, of the University of California at Santa Cruz, also felt that student involvement and critical thinking are crucial. Arguing that transmission of facts is not the main responsibility of the teacher, he quoted a great scholar who told seminar participants, "Gentlemen, the facts are all in the books. In this seminar we will be dealing with more interesting things."

[5] In "The Sins of Higher Education," Smith quotes Woodrow Wilson as saying that "we shall never succeed in creating this organic passion, this great use of the mind . . . until [we] have utterly destroyed the practice of merely formal contact . . . between teacher and pupil," (*Dissenting Opinions* 99). Concluding the essay, Smith writes that

the modern campus is a kind of hell of anxiety that can only be relieved when we speak to our students once more by name and enter into a dialogue with them. The anxiety of note taking, of anonymity, of marks, of examinations, must be transcended before education can replace instruction. This is the only educational task worth doing. (107)

# CHAPTER 7

# Junior Professors and University Service

## Why Worry about It?

MOST ACADEMIC LEADERS are aware of the dangers of excessively involving junior professors in administrative tasks, known as "service" or "university citizenship" at most institutions. Many junior professors enjoy administration and have been exploited by being assigned too much responsibility too early—one of our respondents told of chairing her college's finance committee and arguing with the dean about line items before she had received tenure! Excessive administrative responsibility too early has unquestionably stunted many young faculty members' publishing and teaching.

Reducing junior faculty service responsibilities to zero, however, is also dangerous. While junior professors' participation in service activities should be sensibly limited, senior faculty should not go so far as to advise young professors not to serve on any committees or not to provide any other university administrative service until they receive tenure. One reason is that most junior professors will be expected to provide such service after receiving tenure. It is therefore important for colleagues to acquire some idea of how candidates have performed in those roles before being granted tenure, especially if collegiality and participation in a community of scholars are as important as we think they are.

The second reason is that early professional habits tend to be continued. If bright young professors see that they can get away with slighting all university service responsibilities for six or more years and can be covertly rewarded for their negligence, why should they be expected to change their ways and become model academic citizens after receiving tenure? Several academic leaders among our informants complained about the difficulty of getting committee service from senior colleagues, let alone from junior ones. Institutions need ways to enhance loyalty, not further reduce it.

Third, the right amount of service can combat the anomie and sense of helplessness that plague many junior professors. A few of our junior faculty informants had plenty of time to research but felt isolated from their colleagues, who in turn believed they were obliged to leave the untenured professors alone. One junior professor with an excellent background who had taught several years at a prestigious research university complained:

> The junior professors are thrown too much on their own. You work in total isolation and lose your sense of self-respect. There is no guidance, so you struggle for years finding your niche, your own specialization and place in the department. . . . You have no idea what the others in the department are offering: there's no coordination, not much sense of what's going on.

Further demonstrating the importance of early involvement in service, a good number of senior professors attributed their success to the sense of power and belonging that came from being given reasonable amounts of responsibility in their early years. A department chair at a top research university illustrates this:

> I was terribly lucky in my timing. I'm glad I didn't come through now, when so many of the leading graduate schools are beating down their junior faculty members. . . . [As a young professor] I was a mover and a shaker, got up a committee to bring in Head Start, and served on the state AAUP. I often think what would have happened if I had stayed on at _____ [a prestigious university where junior faculty members have little standing] as a junior professor. I can't imagine it would have been as good.

## What Kind and How Much?
## Women and Minorities at Risk

If we agree that all junior faculty members should have some, but not too much, experience in service assignments, the next question is, What is the right amount? The answer will be different for every campus and perhaps every department. If the department needs some serious administrative effort and the reward criteria will not penalize putting a good fraction of discretionary time into administration, then obviously the young academic could afford a larger commitment to service. Regardless of departmental need, however, it is crucial to understand that substantial devotion to administrative tasks is appropriate only on campuses where the reward criteria will not penalize it. On campuses where only research is rewarded, academic leaders must continue to warn junior professors to accept only the absolute minimum necessary for a sense of belonging.

Not much easier to address is the question of what kind of service is suitable for junior professors. Untenured persons should not chair committees, partly because such positions demand much more time than do other forms of participation and partly because the political requirements are usually beyond the qualifications of most new faculty members. Assigning young professors to campus-wide committees will broaden their perspectives on the institution and help acquaint them with people outside their own departments.[1] Committees on improving writing across the campus serve these two purposes and have the added advantage of acquainting the junior faculty members with local editing and word-processing facilities, as well as refreshing them on the characteristics of good writing. A few seats could be reserved for junior professors in the local faculty senate and on the executive councils of national organizations. Because of teaching and research pressures, many young members of these bodies will learn more than they contribute, but there will be shining exceptions.

Certainly chairs and other mentors must play active parts in advising junior professors and protecting them from excessive commitment in administration, committee work, and other such roles. Requests for service are seldom monitored by a central campus office, so promising young professors often receive more invitations than is wise to accept. The junior faculty members are vulnerable, because they assume more central monitoring than usually occurs and—afraid of offending some powerful voice in a future tenure decision— take on more than they should. Women and minority faculty members are particularly at risk, because conscientious chairs seek the valuable perspectives that they can bring to committees. On every campus we heard this same warning, either from junior professors who had overcommitted themselves in university service or from supervisors who had seen such mistakes.

## Evaluating and Rewarding Service

While academic leaders usually do not and should not put excessive emphasis on service, they should reward reasonable efforts in it and should punish negligence. As mentioned in chapter 3, some of our informants, especially the administrators and junior professors, argued that service should carry more weight in tenure and promotion decisions (see table B, app. 4).

Evaluating service is not difficult. The candidates can list and describe all their administrative and committee responsibilities, and then the relevant supervisors and senior faculty members can provide assessments of the junior professors' contributions.

Service can be rewarded in the same ways that research and teaching are, as discussed in chapter 3. Our experience is that a reasonable involvement in service is intrinsically rewarding as long as the local criteria for formal rewards do not punish service excessively.

## Summary

Junior professors need a minimum involvement in campus service to permit their capabilities in this important aspect of collegiality to be assessed, to initiate them into a significant area of professorial responsibility, and to combat the sense of anomie and helplessness that many junior professors battle. Department chairs should carefully supervise junior faculty involvement in service, however, to ensure that each individual's situation and personality is matched by the right amount and type of activity. Women and minority faculty members need to be particularly encouraged to examine sensibly well-meaning requests that could result in overcommitment.

Service should be assessed at its appropriate value, so that junior professors are neither penalized for good citizenship nor overinvolved in administrative tasks early in their careers.

## NOTE

[1] In a succinct argument for perspective the American poet-essayist Wendell Berry writes, "But to think about only one thing is not to think at all. To think, we have to think about two things and the differences between them" (221).

# CHAPTER 8

# Two Model Junior Faculty Development Programs: A Minimum and a Maximum

ALTHOUGH SEVERAL INSTITUTIONS have begun programs to improve aspects of junior faculty development, few have designed comprehensive approaches. Therefore, the two suggested programs described in this chapter must carry the caveat that neither has been tried out as a whole, although most of the parts have been tried somewhere and seem to make sense. Both programs are fictional, and I use the past tense to avoid the *should*s, *ought*s, and other modal expressions that have infected too much of this book and its kin.[1]

## Bald Knob State University: The Bare Necessities

Times were tough at Bald Knob State University (BKSU), as they had usually been since its founding as a regional agricultural and technical college in 1928. The latest crisis was precipitated by a collapse of the world asbestos market, which sucked in the local asbestos mines and plants, shaking the whole state's economy. The state legislature mandated across-the-board 10% cuts in higher education. Rather than endure more ignominy, thirteen senior professors opted for early retirement, in the same year that an unusually high number—fifteen—reached normal retirement age. Only three of the worst duds on campus wanted to stay on to age seventy.

John Burke Brushfire (also known as "J.B."), vice president of faculty at BKSU, had a problem. His worst fears were confirmed by early reports from the departments on the results of their head-hunting: the lines of hopeful candidates seeking interviews at the professional conventions had shrunk alarmingly, and the number sincerely interested in beginning at BKSU their professional careers in the life of the mind were few indeed. The recruiters, with the exceptions of those in computer science and physical education, felt they would be lucky just to fill each slot: quality would simply have to be left to higher powers. To make matters worse, the student paper—quiescent since the early 1970s—had fastened on to the issue of bad teaching at BKSU like a pit bull and refused to let go. And the commercial media had started to pick it up. A local columnist had learned of Sunny Bozeman's study of leg hairs on tsetse flies in Mozambique and was bent on increasing readership with information on other arcane research projects. The "Teaching Gap" wasn't Watergate or Iranscam, but it had a certain appeal to blue-collar voters tired of annual tuition increases against the background of plant closures.

Vice President Brushfire saw that something would have to be done for junior faculty development if BKSU was not to sink back into the slough of despond in which it had wallowed before he and three others in the academic vice president's group (they called themselves the Scavengers) brought the school up to the edge of respectability by dint of fifty-five-hour weeks, lots of encouragement, a few loyal alumni, and the scrapping of several questionable programs, like the Institute for the Study of Asbestos in Western Thought. Used to making do with next to nothing, the Scavengers knew that this program could not be expensive or require much free time from senior professors already disgruntled with annual exhortations to publish more and teach better.

J.B. sat down with the other Scavengers and sketched out a plan of attack. The first item on the agenda was a quick survey of the criteria employed in the departments when granting tenure, promotion, and other tangible rewards to junior faculty members. No one was surprised when the survey results showed that despite all the paeans to good teaching in BKSU's brochures and catalogs, the criteria were—in every department except English—actually one lone criterion: publications. Teaching was seen as too subjective to measure and service as inappropriate to consider: once in a while a world-class rat might lose a few points on either count if the chair heard too many complaints, but a great publication list would likely offset the disgrace anyhow. One senior dean had groused that Attila the Hun could probably get tenure at BKSU as long as his bio-bib sheet looked good enough.

The Scavengers huddled again and came up with a plan to restore some balance among the traditional three tasks of faculty members, at least of those seeking tenure. After a surprisingly brief discussion in the president's council (composed of the academic vice presidents, the deans, and a few others), J.B. ghosted a memo for the president to send to every dean, department chair, and junior professor: absolutely no one would be considered for tenure or advancement in rank without solid evidence of competence in both scholarship *and teaching* and of at least modest but conscientious participation in college service. Each college could determine the types of evidence admissible, but evidence there would have to be. The memo firmly rejected the myth that publication is a more objective criterion than is teaching (see chapter 3 on this myth) and urged that a variety of means be used to assess teaching quality. Wherever appropriate, student learning should weigh heavily.

Next J.B. and friends considered what sort of minimal program could really assist junior professors to meet the new criteria. They settled on a three-pronged approach: first, a half-day orientation meeting for all new faculty members; second, a program for all department chairs at the next leadership conference showing them how to conduct annual evaluation and planning sessions with junior professors (see the first section of chapter 3); and third—and probably most important—agreement with each dean that establishment of mentoring and other collegial assistance to junior faculty members would be considered one of the most important indications of excellence in the upcoming reviews of colleges and departments. Suggestions to deans and chairs on how to improve such collegiality were also included in the leadership conference (see chapters 5 and 6 for recommendations on collegiality).

The orientation session was not too radical a departure and seemed successful. All new faculty members were firmly told they were expected to attend, and all did attend but one, who was tied up in a dissertation defense. The morning program began with name tags and introductions of newcomers; immediately thereafter J.B. himself introduced campus goals and outlined the new criteria and a few other basic policies. After a break for a Continental breakfast, J.B.'s favorite dean, a down-to-earth local who had a great way with his people, stressed the importance of planning ahead and managing time for balance among research, teaching, and service; finally, one of J.B.'s assistants reviewed the campus resources available to those trying to improve their research and teaching. Plenty of time was allowed for socializing over a light lunch in the slightly seedy Backwoodsman Room of the Student Union, which had to serve in lieu of a faculty club.

The afternoon session presented two engaging young associate professors who had just received tenure. Both were widely known as good teachers and researchers, and their war stories of how they made it included comments on people and practices that had helped them. Both claimed that short but regular blocks of time dedicated to research each week during the academic year had been at least as important as the larger blocks they had wangled once or twice. Both agreed that talking with colleagues about their research and teaching was a big factor in their success so far, although one said that the experience could have been a lot better and that she had needed actively to seek out colleagues and role models.

Whenever J.B. talked with deans during the following year, he made sure that one of the first items to come up was junior faculty development in general and the progress of promising young professors in particular. The next year at the leadership conference, he asked a number of deans and chairs to share success stories about their programs for junior faculty development and for general collegiality. An ardent believer in what he called "MBWA" (Management by Walking Around), J.B. managed to see one or two junior professors at odd moments almost every week and kept up on the progress and problems of at least a sampling of them. The annual orientation sessions and interviews, together with institutional rewards for junior faculty development, became regular features at BKSU.

Not too surprisingly, the number of junior professors who did not make tenure dropped a little each year, partly because departments found it harder and harder to find promising replacements and partly because the new program seemed to catch a few more problems before the point of irreversibility. Of course, some junior professors never made the grade, and some who did left for greener pastures. But there was considerable talk in the halls and around campus coffeepots that the new faculty members were contributing remarkably to campus life and that with the help of these Young Turks, maybe BKSU would make it through the "asbestos crunch" in spite of the boneheads in the administration building.

## Waldorf College: Nothing but the Best

Bertson Martin Worthy III, dean of Waldorf College, was generally pleased but just a bit nervous about his faculty demographics. Looking out his arched window at the wooded hills that had been a large part of Waldorf's charm ever since its founding in the early 1800s, Worthy savored his authorization to hire nearly a dozen new faculty members this year and the prospects for similar numbers in each of the next few years. In a faculty of three hundred, these hirings could make a difference in a hurry. He was glad to have the chance to bring in some fresh blood after having struggled unsuccessfully for three years to placate several decidedly senior faculty members disgruntled by his predecessor's clumsy attempts to make researchers out of faithful teachers who hadn't published word one in twenty years. Although Dean Worthy (Bert to his friends) had a reasonable budget to recruit competitively in the now tight market, one thing worried him: the lack of slots in the last eight years and the outright hiring freeze now ending after two years left him and his colleagues with great expectations but very little experience in hiring new professors or working with them.

The president's ongoing and remarkably successful development campaign among Waldorf's old-money alumni had rightly focused on excellence, and Bert believed that staffing and personnel development were the name of the quality game. The group now retiring included some low-profile types, but by and large the professors he was losing were intensely loyal to Waldorf, and among them were three of his finest teachers and his only world-class scholar in the natural sciences. There could be trouble if the new crop took too long to get up to speed. And speed wasn't the only issue: their direction had to be right. Bert agreed that good teachers had to be good scholars, but the new PhDs he had met at the conventions were certainly a different breed. Those from the best schools saw themselves primarily as specialists—members of an international clan of researchers more at home in the library, in the lab, and at the convention than in the classroom. They were chiefly interested in adding lines to their vitae, because it was their ticket out of any place that they didn't like or that didn't like them. They were not the type to drop over to the faculty club on Thursday evenings for poker or to join him and the president for cocktails after school on Fridays. They gave the distinct impression of being employees—hired guns just passing through—not colleagues savoring membership in a community of seekers and learners.

Clearly, a laissez-faire approach to the new faculty members just would not do. Bert was still mulling his concerns as he joined his usual friends at the faculty club. They had taken lunch together for so long that the group had acquired a quasiformal status. It was a nice mix of present and past administrators, all senior people. Bert felt he got more good advice out of them than he did at more formal meetings. After laying out the problem and successfully countering some crusty types skeptical of development efforts in general, Bert noted a consensus forming: Waldorf needed to do right by the newcomers and set up a model program.

Bert's next move was to stir the Faculty Development Committee, on which he served as an active ex officio member. The committee had done good work in the past but had lost its zip after several years of what some called "the silk-purse gambit," so Bert had replaced a couple of tired members with the best people he could find. At the next meeting, Bert sketched the demographic picture and his dreams, and the members immediately saw the value of working with younger, untenured people rather than older, pricklier ones. Jack Lillienthal quipped that at least "it would be nice to have younger pig's ears for the silk-purse factory." Bert winced and suggested that "teaching younger dogs new tricks" might be a more optimistic metaphor, if not much more complimentary.

A committee member heard through a former sorority sister about an interesting little program for the junior faculty out at Bald Knob State U. A few phone calls to Dean Brushfire established the program's main features. The ideas made a lot of sense to the committee, which decided to adopt and adapt them for Waldorf. The plan wasn't too difficult, since Waldorf was a well-run place; teaching and service had never been completely eliminated from the tenure decisions; development programs, collegiality, and career planning were already components of a number of departments, and Bert had always tried to reward those who fostered such things. But since it never hurts to remind people of good old ideas with new applications, Bert hit these administrative aspects hard at his next meetings with department chairs.

Bert and the Faculty Development Committee talked a few of the best senior and junior professors into helping them. They brainstormed, talked to colleagues, and developed a new program for junior faculty development, which Waldorf implemented the next year.

## *Waldorf's Program*

A year later, as Bert looked back over Waldorf's program, he felt that his people had effectively adapted BKSU's basic administrative program and weekend workshop. BKSU had provided a good first step, and Waldorf's innovations had gone so well that Bert was thinking of writing them up for the next meeting of the Association of American Colleges. These are the main features he had to report:

1. A weekly noon seminar for new professors was held during the fall semester. The program included free luncheon, lasted about ninety minutes, and featured sessions on the following:
   a. Introduction to campus life, including such issues as the library, the computer system, tenure-review details and other campus policies, time management, coping with stress, and health and counseling services.
   b. Basics of college teaching, such as designing a course, model syllabi, techniques for teaching writing and for leading small and large groups, audiovisual services, testing, dealing with cheating, and research on beginning college teachers.
   c. Research strategies and tactics (see chapter 5). Attendance at the research sessions was prerequisite for applying for money to fund travel, research, or curricular development, so nearly all those who were eligible came.
2. A mentoring program for all junior faculty members functioned during the winter semester. Junior professors were paired with compatible senior colleagues—preferably ones who were retiring—on teaching and research projects.[2] In a number of cases mentors from allied departments were assigned. Some senior professors teaching basic courses supervised junior professors teaching other sections of the same courses; other mentors team-taught with junior colleagues; and some pairs just worked on research projects together. All mentors helped their partners develop convincing dossiers for the promotion and tenure decision. The Faculty Development Committee strongly urged the pairs to have regularly scheduled weekly meetings, and it found a little released time or development money for professors who did so. All the mentoring project participants met monthly to discuss their approaches to collaboration.
3. An annual weekend junior faculty retreat on larger issues in college teaching was established. Junior professors were invited after their first full two semesters of teaching. Although the retreat was ostensibly voluntary, attendance was a prerequisite for obtaining curriculum development money. Furthermore, the most promising half of the junior faculty—according to recommendations from their chairs and others—were invited by the dean himself to help organize or otherwise to participate. Held at a great little rustic resort, the retreat offered time to socialize, refreshments, and a number of other features of the Central Pennsylvania Consortium's weekend retreat (see "Some Programs for Improving Junior Faculty Teaching," in chapter 6).
4. Bert and his allies had won agreement from the chairs (despite a few grumblers) to have the faculty handbook amended so that reviews for tenure, promotion, and annual salary increases gave full respect to excellence in nonprint works, in the creation of pedagogical materials, and in research on teaching. Quality would still have to be judged, but good nonprint works and exceptional publications relating to teaching were not to be relegated automatically to second-class status.
5. A junior faculty summer research program was set up to provide a full two-ninths of the regular salary for roughly a third of the junior faculty each summer. The program was competitive, but every junior professor who had a decent research proposal got at least one or two summer stipends during the six years' probation. The program had enough fat in it that junior faculty members with real need could get a greatly reduced teaching loan one semester after the second year on campus. Each individual applying for summer research support was required to attend the noon seminars on research (see item 1).

6. The research office, working with the college committee on writing, set up a free editing service for professors and sponsored short seminars on improving student and faculty writing. Dean Worthy had the committee make sure that every junior faculty member knew of both the service and the seminars.

7. Part of the travel budget was dedicated to the junior faculty. This move was designed to get all junior faculty members out into the "larger networks," as Bert liked to call them, at least every other year, regardless of whether they had papers to give. Bert felt that a good travel budget was an important incentive for ambitious young faculty members: if they felt that being at Waldorf did not cut them off from the rest of the profession, perhaps they would be more apt to stay. Some junior professors used their travel money to get to a library or a lab for the summer.

8. Bert's favorite innovation was the monthly colloquiums. Faculty members from the five institutions within a fifty-mile radius were invited to attend in one of seven discipline groups. Each gathering assembled in a faculty member's home and began with a "bring your own bottle" happy hour, followed by potluck. The evening ended with an assigned review of literature, a work-in-progress report, and discussions. The colloquiums served both social and intellectual functions. Junior faculty members were treated as equals, and several found research collaborators at these "Potluck Symposia," as they were called. The whole thing was started by Bert's Faculty Development Committee, whose main contribution was to plant the idea, to recruit an organizer for each colloquium from one of the five institutions, and to offer secretarial and mailing services to the organizers.

9. With some of the president's development money, Bert was able to buy every junior faculty member a personal computer and hook the computers to the campus mainframe and to BITNET,[3] which gave the professors instant access to electronic mail at campuses all over the Western world. One young molecular biologist almost fainted with joy when he saw a state-of-the-art computer on his desk the first day.

10. A yearlong mentoring and curriculum development program was set up on the Lilly Endowment model (see "Some Programs for Improving Junior Faculty Teaching," in chapter 6) and funded for the first three years by the Syngeld Foundation. The five junior faculty members receiving fellowships were all required to attend a one-week workshop on college teaching with an agenda prepared jointly by the fellows and by professionals in the teaching resource center. The workshop was held at the beginning of July, and no fellow could participate before completing a full two semesters of teaching. All the fellows received financial support for July and August and one class of released time during each of the two semesters following the workshop. During the academic year, as they worked on their projects, the participants all met monthly for lunch. Each team had a professional from the teaching resource center assigned to it, and two of the teams produced first-rate publishable materials. There was extensive publicity about the Syngeld program, and it quickly became a mark of prestige to participate.

11. Any junior faculty member who did not receive a Syngeld fellowship could compete for curriculum development funds. Recipients were required to attend the next weekend retreat on larger issues in college teaching and—if they had not done so already—were taken on a tour of the teaching resource center and assigned a consultant of their choice from the center.

12. To make sure the junior faculty program had a chance of living on after he left, Bert and the Faculty Development Committee arranged for the hiring of a full-time supervisor of faculty development in its broadest definition—support for improved research, teaching, and citizenship. A modest research support staff already existed, and the Faculty Development Committee had a little space and a secretary, so the resources were combined into a single operation directly under the dean's supervision. The new faculty developer was given strict instructions to involve faculty members heavily in the design and delivery of programs, but the professionalism and permanence of the office helped greatly with scheduling, finances, campus communications, and keeping abreast of new ideas at other campuses.

Bert's paper generated more publicity than he really cared to deal with. The other negative effect was that the bigger schools began to snoop around Waldorf, trying to woo away prominent assistant and associate professors. That was a headache, and each case usually ended either in the loss of the desirable faculty member or in a salary increase. Jack Lillienthal kept asking Bert each week whether his program had resulted most recently in brain drain, salary hemorrhage, or "show and tell." Bert would smile wryly and reply that things could be worse.

(For a summary of this chapter, see chapter 9.)

# NOTES

[1] This literary technique has, of course, been used by several authors with utopian visions, notably Sir Thomas More and Edward Bellamy. We hope our more modest proposals work out better in practice than most of More's and Bellamy's have, but since these two brilliant and experienced thinkers made a number of thoroughly bad proposals, there may well be a fly somewhere in our ointment as well. Caveat emptor!

For another, better-written flight into utopian fantasy about education, see Wayne Booth's description in "The Scholar in Society," of Eupaideia, where the schools are organized around a sequence of curiosities and where the National Tax on Verbal Profits—a steeply graduated tax on all publications that make money for author or publisher—drastically reduces the motive for producing what Booth calls "unscholarship."

[2] The idea of pairing junior faculty members with retiring senior colleagues is taken from the Beloit College program funded by the Joyce Foundation, which is described in the section "Some Programs for Improving Junior Faculty Teaching," in chapter 6. The rest of item 2 is based on Boice and Turner's mentoring program at California State University at Long Beach, discussed in chapter 5, under "Tactics for Developing Junior Faculty Scholarship," and in chapter 6, under "Some Programs for Improving Junior Faculty Teaching."

[3] BITNET is an international computer network linking participating academic institutions. It is primarily for electronic mail, but some smaller databases are available through it.

# CHAPTER 9

# Summary and Implications

ONE ACADEMIC PRESIDENT is fond of saying that every evening his university climbs into its cars and drives home. That is his way of emphasizing the faculty as the most important part of any institution of learning. All the rest—the library, the buildings and grounds, the high-profile administrators, the expensive research and teaching equipment—is just support. Institutional quality always has depended and always will depend primarily on the quality of the professors. Of course, the character of the students is also a crucial index of institutional quality, although mediocre schools can seduce fine students for a while with recruiting tricks, scholarships, a good football team, and creative cuisine in the dining centers. But in the long run the best student minds seek out the best faculty mentors. You cannot fool the best students all the time.

If the faculty's primacy in institutional quality is too obvious to require debate, far less clear may be the issue of how faculty quality in an institution can be raised. Conventional practice focuses on careful selection at the point of the tenure decision, leaving development before and after that point to fate and to the true grit of each lonely professor. During the 1970s and early 1980s, it became clear that laissez-faire was insufficient for a large number of senior faculty members, and therefore many institutions established development programs for them. Reviews of these senior faculty development programs have been mixed but generally favorable, and it is now time to increase attention to junior faculty development.

Compared to the business community's exercise of enlightened self-interest in training its employees, higher education's present commitment to employee development is modest indeed. Academia is open to the charge of being penny-wise and pound-foolish in this area. The logical place to increase investment is at the start of an academic career rather than at its middle or end, when self-image and professional habits are well-set. Investments at an early point are more likely to yield the good returns of improved performance and heightened institutional loyalty.

This rationale for junior faculty development is made even more compelling by the demographic facts of academic life. The demand for new faculty members will be abnormally high through the first decade of the twenty-first century, just at a time when the supply and quality of graduate students have diminished in many fields. We in higher education can no longer depend on a large pool of PhDs, like that which enabled institutions in the 1970s and early 1980s to skim off only the best third to half of the job applicants. Selection is cheaper than development, but the days when we could depend exclusively on selection are apparently gone. The danger is that we may repeat the mistakes of the 1950s and 1960s, when the number of positions frequently exceeded the supply, and recruiters pressured to fill slots could not afford to pay too much attention to quality. Faculty worth will suffer in the long run unless university leaders pay more attention to helping their junior professors to develop a variety of talents and to fulfill the range of research, teaching, and administrative tasks needed by the institution. Quality in academic institutions in the United States will depend increasingly on their junior faculty development programs.

## Criteria for Promotion and Tenure

Development programs incongruent with local criteria for promotion and tenure will be exercises in futility. Therefore, as the first step toward junior faculty development, academic leaders should carefully design and communicate the criteria by which junior professors will be rewarded. The reward criteria, together with the development programs, should promote departmental goals in both teaching and research, while not discouraging some minimum appropriate participation in service. Our survey indicated that senior faculty members—including some of the most frequently cited publishing scholars—as well as promising junior professors, generally favor more emphasis on teaching and a little more on service in the allocation of junior faculty rewards. Increasing the role of teaching could result in benefits to society and might actually protect research activities from a public backlash. Increasing the role of service can help reduce anomie and improve junior professors' sense of identification with their institutions.

## Evaluating and Rewarding the Junior Faculty

Evaluation programs should emphasize formative along with summative evaluation: that is, planning for future growth is at least as important as is analyzing past actions for reward. Ideal evaluations are frequent, explicit, and collegial, implying not a hierarchical organization where those at the top require development from hapless victims at the bottom but rather a community of scholars in which all members participate in development. Data sources for evaluations ought to be diverse and representative.

We can properly require scholarship—keeping up in the field—of every faculty member, but we should remember that it is distinct from research and publication. We can evaluate and reward the scholarship and research of some talented individuals who publish infrequently, and it might be advisable to limit the number of published pages that junior professors may submit for the tenure review.

Teaching can and should be evaluated with at least as much objectivity as research is, but to do so will require data in addition to evaluations by current students. Such means include standardized-test results, peer evaluation, post hoc student evaluation, and examination of syllabi and tests. They all cost something, but so does evaluation of publication. Our failure to pay those costs sends a clearer signal about our real values than do all our pieties about the importance of teaching.

The tangible rewards of tenure, promotion, and salary will continue to play a central role in junior faculty reward systems, but some adjustments to conventional practices may increase the effectiveness of each as an incentive. These adjustments could include hiring more carefully in order to tenure a larger fraction of the junior faculty, promoting in small steps within rank, communicating clearly the meaning of salary increases, rewarding through research grants rather than through salary increases, and rewarding groups rather than individuals for achievements.

Intangible rewards, however, such as the encouragement and trust provided by administrators, colleagues, and family, probably represent the most powerful incentives over the long run for junior as well as senior faculty effort. Our most effective aid to our junior colleagues may consist of improving their sense of belonging to a caring community of scholars.

# Preparing the Dossier

No single event hangs over junior professors' heads like the tenure and promotion decision at the end of five or six years' employment. To a frightening extent, this verdict and thus their professional fates depend on the quality of their dossiers. This collection of documents—intended to present the merits of the candidate to several impersonal and critical committees—requires time, thought, and care; the candidate, together with colleagues, should begin gathering data for tenure and promotion reviews soon after being hired. Senior professors who assist a junior colleague in putting together a dossier can offer their mature judgment and reduce the candidate's need to indulge in self-promotion.

Dossiers should present a wide range of appropriate data on candidates' scholarship, teaching, and service, all attractively presented and organized to emphasize the achievements that are significant in the light of local criteria. The dossier should be nicely bound, with tabs, headings, a table of contents, and other devices to provide reviewers easy access to important data and conclusions.

# Developing Research Skills

Programs to develop junior faculty research skills are clearly needed to ensure institutional quality, for a number of reasons. The habit of research and writing must be established early if it is ever to be established. Furthermore, first employment positions seem to affect researchers' later careers even more than do the graduate schools they attended. Finally, institutions cannot assume that the supply of young researchers will always meet future demands.

Our interviews resulted in useful findings about academic research and generally support the conclusions of other writers. First, research is not usually a lone effort that happens spontaneously in private but is largely a product of "evocative environments" in a community of scholars. Effective programs for junior professors are characterized by firm administrative support, good management, good communication, an orientation toward the future, and, especially, collegiality. The tools for developing junior faculty research skills include mentoring programs, group projects, funds for travel to interact with the larger community of scholars, research funding, good facilities and equipment, and appropriate—not excessive—amounts of time for research.

Experienced researchers in both the sciences and the humanities agree that ideas for research projects come either from direct, personal conversation with other scholars or from the imagined dialogue that a scholar pursues through questioning, critical reading.

Most productive scholars in a variety of fields are able to research and write in short, regularly scheduled blocks of time. While the majority of scholars in the humanities still take notes, a significant minority do not. Those who dispense with notes write or mentally compose outlines or drafts early in their research; then as they read they compare each passage with the drafts, revising their ideas as they proceed. A large fraction of scholars who take notes do not use cards but use computers, photocopiers, or full sheets of paper. The note takers usually read their notes over, arrange them carefully, and write directly from their files.

Successful publishing scholars advise that a junior professor carefully select publishers with interests similar to the area covered by the manuscript, use personal contacts to help select and approach publishers, submit cover letters and abstracts or sample chapters to several publishers at once and regard rejection from most as normal, and—to break into print—first try the university presses or scholarly journals.

## Developing Teaching Skills

Programs for improving junior faculty teaching are needed because many young professors are poorly prepared to teach. Furthermore, such programs validate teaching as a topic of campus conversation, demonstrate institutional support for teaching, and acquaint faculty members with the literature on teaching.

Our survey of junior faculty instructional development turned up a number of interesting programs, such as those sponsored by Beloit College, the Central Pennsylvania Consortium, universities in Great Britain, the Great Lakes

Colleges Association, and the Lilly Endowment. The key principles in all these programs include collegiality, administrative support, prestige, faculty owner-ship, intellectual challenge, and interdisciplinarity. The specific means for improving junior faculty teaching include mentoring, curriculum development projects, group projects (classes, workshops, retreats), scheduling the program only after the first year, and the use of teaching consultants, resource centers, intervisitation, and advice from students.

Our informants believed that junior professors should be helped to realize that the quantity of facts conveyed is not the only factor in good teaching. Among other elements are orderliness, clarity, humor, enthusiasm, the ability to stimulate student involvement and new modes of thinking, and rapport with students.

## Developing Administrative Skills

Junior professors should have a minimum involvement in campus service to enable their capabilities in this important aspect of collegiality to be assessed, to initiate them into a significant area of professorial responsibility, and to combat the sense of anomie and helplessness that many junior professors battle. Department chairs should carefully supervise junior faculty involvement in service, however, to ensure that each individual's situation and personality is matched by the right amount and type of activity. Women and minority faculty members need to be particularly encouraged to assess sensibly well-meaning requests that could result in overcommitment.

Service should be evaluated frequently so that it is given its appropriate due and so that junior professors are neither penalized for good citizenship nor overinvolved in administrative tasks early in their careers.

## Model Programs: A Minimum and an Ideal

A minimal program of junior faculty development would include the following features:

- Adjustment of the criteria for tenure, advancement, and merit pay to reflect the long-run goals of the institution. In many cases, this will mean more attention to teaching and service.
- Instruction to department chairs on meeting with junior faculty members for annual assessment and planning interviews that emphasize future development.
- Agreement among top administrators to reward efforts promoting collegiality and junior faculty development at college and depart-ment levels.
- A five-hour basic junior faculty orientation session held before classes begin in the fall or during the early part of the semes-

ter. The program would acquaint new professors with the campus, its goals and basic policies; outline the criteria and procedures for attaining tenure and advancement; describe campus programs and resources for helping candidates meet the criteria; and provide time for new professors to socialize with one another.

An ideal program of junior faculty development might have the following aspects, in addition to everything in the preceding list:

- A weekly noon seminar for new professors held during the fall or winter semester of the first year after hiring. The program, which would include free luncheon, would last about ninety minutes and feature any of the topics listed below.
- Sessions on strategies and tactics for teaching, the basic subjects of which might include designing a course, techniques for teaching writing and for leading small and large groups, audiovisual services, testing, dealing with cheating, and research on beginning college teachers.
- Sessions on research strategies and tactics, held no later than the first part of the winter semester. Attendance could be prerequisite to any application for funding of research, travel, or curriculum development.
- Sessions on university life, including such issues as the library, the computer system, tenure-review details, time management, coping with stress, and health and counseling services.
- A mentoring program for all junior faculty members. Each mentor and protégé would meet weekly, and all participants would assemble monthly.
- Amendment of the criteria for publication quality to allow credit for excellent pedagogical materials and research on teaching and learning.
- An annual weekend retreat on larger issues in college teaching held for those who have completed two semesters of teaching.
- Summer research support or released time during another academic period.
- A free editing service and short seminars on improving writing skills.
- A generous travel budget for the junior faculty.
- Discipline-centered colloquiums held in the evening at faculty members' homes.
- Up-to-date microcomputers—connected to the campus mainframe and to BITNET—for each junior faculty member.
- A yearlong curriculum development and mentoring program based on the Lilly Endowment model for selected junior faculty members.

- Curriculum development funds for anyone not chosen for the yearlong program.
- Appointment of a university officer with adequate space and staff to supervise faculty development in its broadest definition—support for improved scholarship, teaching, and citizenship.

## Implications for Further Research

Nearly every aspect of junior faculty development deserves further scrutiny.

Faculty demographics in each field could be surveyed in more detail. Bowen and Sosa have made a splendid first cut of the question, but their survey seldom divides areas into categories more narrow than, for example, "humanities" or "biology." Such broad divisions necessarily obscure considerable differences among subfields, so professional associations could appropriately examine and publish their own demographics to help academic leaders and counselors understand which areas are going to experience the sharpest increases in demand for new faculty members and which have experienced the greatest dips in graduate school enrollment. Communicating this information in a timely fashion to undergraduates may prove beneficial to the whole enterprise by reducing the current vulnerability of academic hiring to boom-and-bust cycles. It would be especially important to tell such information to underrepresented minorities to help reverse their present lamentable exodus from academia.

Another area to study would be the short- and long-term effects of each junior faculty program component on participants and institutions. Similarly, it would be interesting to compare how efforts to promote junior faculty development are organized at various institutions and to contrast their cost-effectiveness in differing settings. An important question in the delivery of such programs is whether they should be centralized or assigned to departments; an Australian report suggests that development of research skills is best divided among departments but that development of teaching can be more centralized (Moses).

A valuable tangent for continued study would be the long-term effects of reward criteria that emphasize good teaching. One study found that some teaching-oriented institutions, among them the University of California at Santa Cruz, had unusually high numbers of undergraduates who continued into graduate work (Fuller). Knapp and Goodrich reached similar conclusions in an extensive study of the backgrounds of American scientists (reported in Smith, *Killing* 86–87). Further substantiation of these findings could hearten the academic leaders considering greater emphasis on teaching in their criteria for rewards of junior as well as senior faculty members.

The aspect of costs is intriguing: what are the immediate and long-run costs of research-oriented reward criteria? Certainly the top research universities bring in a large fraction of their incomes from research, but has this benefit been overrated, especially for middle-ranking research institutions?

A number of universities have begun recently to increase undergraduate involvement in research. Does this trend have any important ramifications for junior faculty development? Could marrying teaching more thoroughly to research offer institutions a way of skirting the teaching-versus-research quandary and result in both better teaching and better research?

## Concluding Note

A great deal can be done in the area of junior faculty development with a very modest capital outlay; the main requisite is vision. We agree with the report on the Lilly Endowment junior faculty program: "Lack of imagination, initiative, and drive—not lack of money—accounts for the failure of institutions to concern themselves with the development of their junior scholars into senior professors" (Bornholdt 2).

Leaders who have that vision will recognize that societal issues make this area one of the most pressing and far-reaching of all the matters they have to deal with. Academic decision makers cannot shut their eyes to the effects of their policies on the whole society. Wayne Booth expresses it well:

> Whatever happens to our society, we cannot afford to spend any time proclaiming our helplessness before its forces. As one of the most powerful of society's "estates," we can be sure that whatever conditions we find in the world as we continue our efforts at scholarship have been to a surprising degree of our own making. In what we write, and perhaps even more in what we teach, we make the society in which we shall continue to remake ourselves. (140)

# Works Cited and Consulted

Alfonsi, Alice. "Teaching Professors to Teach." *New York Times Education Summer Survey* 18 Aug. 1985: 33.

American Council on Education. *American Universities and Colleges.* 12th ed. New York: Gruyter, 1983.

Association of American Colleges. *Integrity in the College Curriculum: A Report to the Academic Community.* Washington: Assn. of Amer. Colls., 1985.

Atkinson, Dorothy. "Soviet and East European Studies in the United States." *Slavic Review* 47 (1988): 397–413.

Bailiff, John, and Susan Kahn. "The University and the Rediscovery of Teaching: A System-Level Model." Kurfiss et al. 6: 75–103.

Baldwin, Roger G., ed. *Incentives for Faculty Vitality.* New Directions for Higher Education 51. San Francisco: Jossey-Bass, 1985.

Baldwin, Roger G., and Marsha V. Krotseng. "Incentives in the Academy: Issues and Options." Baldwin 5–20.

Barber, Sandra Powell. "Faculty Development Needs as a Function of Status in the Academic Guild." Kurfiss et al. 6: 33–40.

Bayer, Allan E., and Jeffrey E. Dutton. "Career Age and Research-Professional Activities of Academic Scientists." *Journal of Higher Education* 48 (1977): 259–82.

Beeman, Alice L. *Toward Better Teaching: A Report on the Post-doctoral Teaching Awards Program of the Lilly Endowment, Inc., September 1974–August 1980.* Indianapolis: Lilly Endowment, [c. 1981].

Bellah, Robert N., et al. *Habits of the Heart.* New York: Harper, 1985.

Bennett, William J. *To Reclaim a Legacy.* Washington: NEH, 1984.

Berger, Thomas. Qtd. in advertisement for the Writing Laboratory. Univ. of Illinois, Chicago, Nov. 1986.

Berry, Wendell. "Two Economies." *Review and Expositor* 81 (1984): 209–23.

Bess, James L., ed. *Motivating Professors to Teach Effectively.* New Directions for Teaching and Learning 10. San Francisco: Jossey-Bass, 1982.

Blackburn, Robert T. "Faculty Career Development: Theory and Practice." Clark and Lewis 55–85.

Bogue, E. Grady, and Wayne Brown. "Performance Incentives for State Colleges." *Harvard Business Review* Nov.–Dec. 1982: 123–28.

Boice, Robert. "Coping with Difficult Colleagues." *Department Advisor* 2.4 (1987): 5–8.

———. "Is Released Time an Effective Component of Faculty Development Programs?" *Research in Higher Education* 26 (1987): 311–26.

———. *Professors as Writers: A Self-Help Guide to Productive Writing.* Stillwater: New Forums, 1990.

———. "Reexamination of Traditional Emphases in Faculty Development." *Research in Higher Education* 21 (1984): 195–209.

Boice, Robert, and Jim L. Turner. "Faculty Developers as Facilitators of Scholarly Writing." Kurfiss et al. 6: 103–14.

———. "The FIPSE-CSULB Mentoring Project for New Faculty." Kurfiss et al. 8: 117–39.

Bok, Derek. *Higher Learning.* Cambridge: Harvard UP, 1986.

Booth, Wayne C. "The Scholar in Society." Gibaldi 116–43.

Bornholdt, Laura. Introduction. Beeman 1–5.

Bowen, Howard R., and Jack H. Schuster. *American Professors: A National Resource Imperiled.* New York: Oxford UP, 1986.

Bowen, William G. "The Junior Faculty: A Time for Understanding and Support." *Change* July–Aug. 1984: 22-31.

Bowen, William G., and Julie Ann Sosa. *Prospects for Faculty in the Arts and Sciences: A Study of Factors Affecting Demand and Supply, 1987 to 2012.* Princeton: Princeton UP, 1989.

Boyer, Ernest L. *College: The Undergraduate Experience in America.* New York: Harper, 1987.

Bracey, Gerald W. "The Time Has Come to Abolish Research Journals: Too Many Are Writing Too Much about Too Little." *Chronicle of Higher Education* 25 Mar. 1987: 44.

Braskamp, Larry A., Dale C. Brandenburg, and John C. Ory. *Evaluating Teaching Effectiveness: A Practical Guide.* Beverly Hills: Sage, 1984.

Brown, Abby. "Career Development 1986: A Look at Trends and Issues." *Personnel Administrator* Mar. 1986: 45–109.

"Campus Research." *Wall Street Journal* 29 Nov. 1985, sec. 2: 15.

Cargill, Oscar, William Charvat, and Donald D. Walsh. *The Publication of Academic Writing.* New York: MLA, 1966.

Cartter, A. A. *An Assessment of Quality in Graduate Education.* Washington: Amer. Council on Educ., 1966.

Centra, John A. "Maintaining Faculty Vitality through Faculty Development." Clark and Lewis 141–56.

Centra, John, et al. *A Guide to Evaluating Teaching for Promotion and Tenure.* Syracuse: Center for Instructional Dev., Syracuse U, 1987.

Christy, Howard. Personal note. May 1989.

Clark, Burton R. *Academic Life in America: Different Worlds.* Princeton: Carnegie Foundation for the Advancement of Teaching, 1987.

Clark, Shirley M., and Darrell R. Lewis, eds. *Faculty Vitality and Institutional Productivity: Critical Perspectives for Higher Education.* New York: Teachers Coll. P, Columbia U, 1985.

Cole, Jonathan R., and Harriet Zuckerman. "The Productivity Puzzle: Persistence and Change in Patterns of Publication of Men and Women Scientists." *Advances in Motivation and Achievement*. Ed. Marjorie W. Steinkemp and Martin L. Maehr. Vol. 2. Greenwich: JAI, 1984. 217–58.

Conference Board of Associated Research Councils. *An Assessment of Research-Doctorate Programs in the United States*. 5 vols. Washington: Natl. Acad., 1982.

Conrad, Clifton F., and Robert T. Blackburn. "Program Quality in Higher Education: A Review and Critique of Literature and Research." *Higher Education: Handbook of Theory and Research* 1 (1985): 283–308.

Creswell, John W. *Faculty Research Performance: Lessons from the Sciences and the Social Sciences*. ASHE-ERIC Higher Education Report 4. Washington: Assn. for the Study of Higher Educ., 1985.

Dalton, Gene, and Paul Thompson. *Novations: Strategies for Career Management*. Glenview: Scott, 1986.

Devens, Monica S., and Nancy J. Bennett. "The MLA Surveys of Foreign Language Graduate Programs, 1984–85." *ADFL Bulletin* 17.3 (1986): 19–27.

Diamond, Nancy A. "Dean's Seminars for New Faculty at the University of Illinois." Conference of the Professional and Organizational Dev. Network in Higher Educ. Jekyll Island, GA, 5–8 Oct. 1989.

Donald, Janet G. "The State of Research on University Teaching Effectiveness." *Using Research to Improve Teaching*. Ed. Janet G. Donald and Arthur M. Sullivan. New Directions for Teaching and Learning 23. San Francisco: Jossey-Bass, 1985. 7–25.

Eble, Kenneth, and Wilbert J. McKeachie. *Improving Undergraduate Education through Faculty Development*. San Francisco: Jossey-Bass, 1986.

Eiduson, Bernice. *Scientists: Their Psychological World*. New York: Basic, 1962.

Erikson, Erik H. "Growth and Crisis of the Healthy Personality." *Identity and the Life Cycle*. Psychological Issues 1.1. New York: Intl. UP, 1959. 50–100.

Eurich, Nell P. *Corporate Classrooms: The Learning Business*. Princeton: Carnegie Foundation for the Advancement of Teaching, 1985.

Evangelauf, Jean. "Lengthening of Time to Earn a Doctorate Causes Concern." *Chronicle of Higher Education* 15 Mar. 1989: 1+.

"Faculty Notes: Tenure Rate for Men and Women." *Chronicle of Higher Education* 29 Mar. 1989: A17.

Ferruolo, Stephen C. *The Origins of the University: The Schools of Paris and Their Critics, 1100–1215*. Stanford: Stanford UP, 1985.

Fink, L. Dee. *The First Year of College Teaching*. New Directions for Teaching and Learning 17. San Francisco: Jossey-Bass, 1984.

———. "Oklahoma's Professional Development Seminar: An Assessment of Its First Year." Conference of the Professional and Organizational Dev. Network in Higher Educ. Jekyll Island, GA, 5–8 Oct. 1989.

Fitzpatrick, Tim. "U. Research Proponents Take Case to Lawmakers." *Salt Lake Tribune* 30 Apr. 1989: A3.

Foster, Stephen F., and J. Gordon Nelson. "Teaching Improvement in Canada: Data concerning What and How." *Canadian Journal of Higher Education* 5 Aug. 1987: 120–25.

French-Lazovik, Grace. *Practices That Improve Teaching Evaluation.* New Directions for Teaching and Learning 11. San Francisco: Jossey-Bass, 1982.

Fuller, Carol H. "Ph.D. Recipients: Where Did They Go to College?" *Change* Nov.–Dec. 1986: 42-51.

Gaff, Jerry G. *Toward Faculty Renewal.* San Francisco: Jossey-Bass, 1975.

Ghiselin, Brewster. *The Creative Process.* Berkeley: U of California P, 1952.

Gibaldi, Joseph, ed. *Introduction to Scholarship in Modern Languages and Literatures.* New York: MLA, 1981.

Glaser, Barney G., and Anselm L. Strauss. *The Discovery of Grounded Theory: Strategies for Qualitative Research.* Hawthorne: Aldine, 1967.

Glitzer, Barbara M., and Barbara Maher. "Six Steps to Contemporary Career Development." *Training/HRD* Dec. 1982: 48+.

Goldstein, Amy J. *Graduate Programs in the Humanities and Social Sciences 1987.* 21st ed. Princeton: Peterson's, 1987.

Hardy, Kenneth. "Social Origins of American Scientists and Scholars." *Science* 9 Aug. 1974: 497–506.

Harris, John S. *Teaching Technical Writing: A Pragmatic Approach.* Tuscaloosa: Assn. of Teachers of Technical Writing (c/o Donald H. Cunningham), Auburn U, 1989.

Hart, Edward L. *God's Spies: The Scholar's Call.* Provo: Coll. of Humanities, Brigham Young U, 1983.

Hauck, Robert J-P. "Ph.D. Enrollments Continue to Decline." *PS* 27.1 (1984): 79.

Hiedemann, Robert E., ed. *The American Future and the Humane Tradition: The Role of the Humanities in Higher Education.* N.p.: Associated Faculty, 1982.

Hintz, John A. "Before Trying Enrollment-Management Techniques, Colleges Should Assess Their Own Academic Quality." *Chronicle of Higher Education* 13 May 1987: 96.

Hipps, G. Melvin. "Talking about Teaching: The Contributions of Senior Faculty to Junior Faculty." Nelsen and Siegel 43–48.

Huber, Bettina J., et al. "MLA Surveys of PhD Placement: Most Recent Findings and Decade-long Trends." *ADFL Bulletin* 20.3 (1989): 20–30.

Hughes, R. M. *A Study of the Graduate Schools in America.* Oxford: Miami UP, 1925.

Hynes, William J. "Strategies for Faculty Development." *Leadership Roles of Chief Academic Officers.* Ed. David G. Brown. New Directions for Higher Education 47. San Francisco: Jossey-Bass, 1984. 31–38.

Ilf, Ilya Arnoldovich, and Evgeniy Petrov. "Kolumb prichalivaet k beregu." *Sobranie sochineniva.* Ed. A. G. Dementev, V. P. Kataev, and K. M. Simonov. Vol. 3. Moscow: Gosudarstvennoe izdatelstvo khodozhestvennoi literatury, 1961. 73–81. 5 vols.

Jarvis, Donald K., William Reger IV, and Glen C. Worthey. "Development and Incentives for General Education Faculty." *Improving University Teaching: Contributed Papers II.* Proc. of 12th intl. conference. Heidelberg, Ger., 15-18 July 1986. College Park: U of Maryland U Coll.; Heidelberg: U of Heidelberg, 1986. 399–409.

Jencks, Christopher, and David Riesman. *The Academic Revolution.* Garden City: Doubleday, 1968.

"Job Conditions for Writing Instructors Called 'Fundamentally Unfair.'" *Chronicle of Higher Education* 1 Apr. 1987: 13.

Kerr, Steven. "On the Folly of Rewarding A, While Hoping for B." *Academy of Management Journal* 18 (1975): 769–83.

Kirschling, Wayne J. "Conceptual Problems and Issues in Academic Labor Productivity." Lewis and Becker 129–30.

Knapp, R. H., and H. B. Goodrich. *Origins of American Scientists.* Chicago: U of Chicago P, 1952.

Kocis, Robert A. "How Colleges Should Hire Faculty Members: Recruit in Slow Fields, Not Hot Ones." *Chronicle of Higher Education* 25 Mar. 1987: 44–45.

Kram, K. E., and L. A. Isabella. "Mentoring Alternatives: The Role of Peer Relationships in Career Development." *Academy of Management Journal* 28 (1985): 110–32.

Kurfiss, Joan, et al., eds. *To Improve the Academy: Resources for Student, Faculty, and Institutional Development.* Vols. 6–8. Stillwater: New Forums, 1987–89.

LaNoue, George R., and Barbara A. Lee. *Academics in Court: The Consequences of Faculty Discrimination Litigation.* Ann Arbor: U of Michigan P, 1987.

Lehman, Harvey C. *Age and Achievement.* Princeton: Princeton UP, 1953.

Lewis, Darrell R., and William E. Becker, Jr., eds. *Academic Rewards in Higher Education.* Cambridge: Ballinger, 1979.

Lewis, Karen. "New Faculty Teaching/Orientation Seminar." Conference of the Professional and Organizational Dev. Network in Higher Educ. Jekyll Island, GA, 5–8 Oct. 1989.

Light, Donald, Jr. "Thinking about Faculty." *Daedalus* 103 (1974): 258–64.

Mandell, Richard D. *The Professor Game.* Garden City: Doubleday, 1977.

McKeachie, Wilbert J. "Financial Incentives Are Ineffective for Faculty." Lewis and Becker 3–20.

McMillen, Liz. "Faculty Development Programs Seen Often Marginal to Important Campus Needs." *Chronicle of Higher Education* 15 Apr. 1987: 15–16.

———. "The Residue from Academics' Lawsuits: Often Anguish for Everyone Involved." *Chronicle of Higher Education* 1 Apr. 1987: 1+

Michalak, Stanley J., Jr. "Enhancing Critical-Thinking Skills in Traditional Liberal Arts Courses: Report on a Faculty Workshop." *Liberal Education* 72 (1986): 253–62.

Millman, Jason, ed. *Handbook of Teacher Evaluation.* Beverly Hills: Sage, Natl. Council on Measurement in Educ., 1981.

"MLA Doctoral Survey: Foreign Languages, Comparative Literature, and Linguistics." *ADFL Bulletin* 9.3 (1978): 1–2.

Mooney, Carolyn J. "Uncertainty Is Rampant As Colleges Begin to Brace for Faculty Shortage Expected to Begin in 1990's." *Chronicle of Higher Education* 25 Jan. 1989: A14–A17.

More, Thomas. *Utopia.* Trans. Paul Turner. New York: Penguin, 1965.

Morrill, Paul Hampton, and Emil R. Spees. *The Academic Profession: Teaching in Higher Education.* New York: Human Sciences, 1982.

Moses, Ingrid. "Academic Development Units and the Improvement of Teaching." *Higher Education* 14 (1985): 75–100.

Nelsen, William C. "Faculty Development: Perceived Needs for the 1980's." Nelsen and Siegel 145–49.

———. *Renewal of the Teacher Scholar: Faculty Development in the Liberal Arts College.* Washington: Assn. of Amer. Colls., 1980.

Nelsen, William C., and Michael E. Siegel. *Effective Approaches to Faculty Development.* Washington: Assn. of Amer. Colls., 1980.

Newman, Frank. *Higher Education and the American Resurgence.* Princeton: Carnegie Foundation for the Advancement of Teaching, 1985.

Nordvall, Robert C. *The Process of Change in Higher Education Institutions.* AAHE-ERIC/Higher Education Research Report 7. Washington: Amer. Assn. for Higher Educ., 1982.

Painton, Priscilla. "Troubled Times for Tenure." *Time* 26 Feb. 1990: 72.

Pelz, Donald, and Frank Andrews. *Scientists in Organizations: Productive Climates for Research and Development.* Rev. ed. Ann Arbor: Inst. of Social Research, 1976.

"Professional Development: Bringing New Faculty on Board." *Academic Leader* Aug. 1986: 1–2. (Published monthly by Magna Publications, 2718 Dryden Dr., Madison, WI 53704.)

Rausch, Diane K., Bonnie P. Ortiz, Robin A. Douthitt, and Laurie L. Reed. "The Academic Revolving Door: Why Do Women Get Caught?" *College and University Personnel Association Journal* 40 (1989): 1–16.

Reskin, Barbara F. "Scientific Productivity and the Reward Structure of Science." *American Sociological Review* 42 (1977): 491–504.

Roe, Ann. *A Psychological Study of Eminent Psychologists and Anthropologists, and a Comparison with Biological and Physical Scientists.* Psychological Monographs 67.2. New York: Amer. Psychological Assn., 1953.

Roose, K. D., and C. J. Anderson. *A Rating of Graduate Programs.* Washington: Amer. Council on Educ., 1970.

Ross, Aden. "Tenure or the Great Chain of Being." *Change* July–Aug. 1987: 54–55.

Schuster, Jack H. "Faculty Vitality: Observations from the Field." Baldwin 21–32.

Schuster, Jack H., and Howard R. Bowen. "The Faculty at Risk." *Change* Sept.–Oct. 1985: 12–21.

Schwen, Thomas M., and Mary Deane Sorcinelli. "A Profile of a Postdoctoral Teaching Program." *Revitalizing Teaching through Faculty Development.* Ed. P. A. Lacey. New Directions for Teaching and Learning 15. San Francisco: Jossey-Bass, 1983. 81–94.

Seldin, Peter. *Teaching Professors to Teach: Case Studies and Methods of Faculty Development in British Universities Today.* Croton-on-Hudson: Blythe-Pennington, 1977.

Sheehy, Gail. *Passages.* New York: Bantam, 1976.

Siegel, Michael E. "Empirical Findings on Faculty Development Programs." Nelsen and Siegel 131–44.

Smelser, Neil J. *Lower Division Education in the University of California: A Report from the Task Force on Lower Division Education.* Berkeley: U of California, 1986.

Smith, Page. *Dissenting Opinions: Selected Essays.* San Francisco: North Point, 1984.

————. *Killing the Spirit: Higher Education in America.* New York: Viking, 1990.

Snow, C. P. *The Two Cultures and a Second Look: An Expanded Version of* The Two Cultures and the Scientific Revolution. Cambridge: Cambridge UP, 1964.

Sorcinelli, Mary Deane. "Satisfactions and Concerns of New University Teachers." Kurfiss et al. 7: 121-33.

*Statistical Abstract of the United States 1986.* 106th ed. Washington: U. S. Dept. of Commerce, Bureau of the Census, 1986.

Study Group on the Conditions of Excellence in Higher Education. *Involvement in Learning: Realizing the Potential of American Higher Education.* Washington: U. S. Dept. of Educ., 1984.

Sykes, Charles J. *ProfScam: Professors and the Demise of Higher Education.* New York: St. Martin's, 1988.

Thoreau, Henry David. *Walden: Or, Life in the Woods.* New York: NAL, 1960.

Thorndike, E. L. "The Origin of Superior Men." *Scientific Monthly* May 1943: 424-33.

Thurow, Lester C. "A Surge in Inequality." *Scientific American* May 1987: 30-37.

Toynbee, Arnold J. *A Study of History.* London: Oxford UP, 1946.

Tuchman, Barbara Wertheim. *The March of Folly: From Troy to Vietnam.* New York: Knopf, 1984.

Turner, Jim L., and Robert Boice. "A Longitudinal Study of Faculty Careers." Meeting of the Western Psychological Assn. Long Beach, CA, 25 Apr. 1987.

————. "Starting at the Beginning: The Concerns and Needs of New Faculty." Kurfiss et al. 6: 41-55.

Veblen, Thorstein. *The Higher Learning in America.* 1918. New York: Hill, 1957.

Visher, S. S. *Scientists Starred 1903-43 in* American Men of Science: *A Study of Collegiate and Doctoral Training, Birthplace, Distribution, Backgrounds, and Developmental Influences.* Baltimore: Johns Hopkins UP, 1947.

Watkins, Beverly T. "Colleges Are Said to Offer Little Help to Senior Professors." *Chronicle of Higher Education* 29 Mar. 1989: A17.

Williams, Lea E. "The Plight of Junior Faculty at Black Private Colleges." *Journal of the National Association of Women Deans, Administrators, and Counselors* 48.2 (1985): 12-18.

Woodring, Paul. *The Higher Learning in America: A Reassessment.* New York: McGraw, 1968.

Wylie, Neil R., and Jon W. Fuller. "Enhancing Faculty Vitality through Collaboration among Colleagues." Baldwin 99-108.

Zanna, Mark P., and John M. Darley, eds. *The Compleat Academic: A Practical Guide for the Beginning Social Scientist.* New York: Random, 1987.

Zuckerman, Harriet. *Scientific Elite: Nobel Laureates in the United States.* New York: Free, 1977.

# APPENDIX 1

# Information Sources for Junior Faculty Development

## BOOKS

### Career Advice for Junior Faculty Members

Boice, Robert. *Professors as Writers: A Self-Help Guide to Productive Writing.* Stillwater: New Forums, 1990.

Zanna, Mark P., and John M. Darley, eds. *The Compleat Academic: A Practical Guide for the Beginning Social Scientist.* New York: Random, 1987. (This handbook contains chapters on getting hired, managing a career, departmental politics, teaching, research, advising, applying for grants, publishing, and researching outside academia. Most sections are useful to junior professors in any field.)

### Development of Teaching

Eble, Kenneth, and Wilbert J. McKeachie. *Improving Undergraduate Education through Faculty Development.* San Francisco: Jossey-Bass, 1986.

Nelsen, William C., and Michael E. Siegel. *Effective Approaches to Faculty Development.* Washington: Assn. of Amer. Colls., 1980.

### Educational Technology

Graves, William H., ed. *Computing across the Curriculum: Academic Perspectives.* McKinney: Academic Computing, 1989. (Since adequate mentoring on educational technology is often hard to arrange, junior professors may need resources such as this book.)

### Evaluation of Teaching

Braskamp, Larry A., Dale C. Brandenburg, and John C. Ory. *Evaluating Teaching Effectiveness: A Practical Guide.* Beverly Hills: Sage, 1984.

Centra, John, et al. *A Guide to Evaluating Teaching for Promotion and Tenure.* Syracuse: Center for Instructional Dev., Syracuse U, 1987.

### Faculty Incentives

Baldwin, Roger G., ed. *Incentives for Faculty Vitality.* New Directions for Higher Education 51. San Francisco: Jossey-Bass, 1985.

### Research Performance

Creswell, John W. *Faculty Research Performance: Lessons from the Sciences and the Social Sciences.* ASHE-ERIC Higher Education Report 4. Washington: Assn. for the Study of Higher Educ., 1985.

Zuckerman, Harriet. *Scientific Elite: Nobel Laureates in the United States.* New York: Free, 1977.

### The State of the Professoriat

Bowen, Howard R., and Jack H. Schuster. *American Professors: A National Resource Imperiled.* New York: Oxford UP, 1986.

Bowen, William G., and Julie Ann Sosa. *Prospects for Faculty in the Arts and Sciences: A Study of Factors Affecting Demand and Supply, 1987 to 2012.* Princeton: Princeton UP, 1989.

### Support for Junior Faculty Members

Boice, Robert. *Supporting the Development of New Faculty.* San Francisco: Jossey-Bass, 1992.

Bowen, William G. "The Junior Faculty: A Time for Understanding and Support." *Change* July–Aug. 1984: 22-31.

# PERIODICALS

*To Improve the Academy: Resources for Student, Faculty, and Institutional Development.* (This annual publication of the Professional and Organizational Development Network in Higher Education is available from New Forums Press, P.O. Box 876, Stillwater, OK 74076.)

*The Journal of Staff, Program, and Organizational Development.* (This quarterly publication is affiliated with four national organizations dealing with development. It can be ordered through New Forums Press, P.O. Box 876, Stillwater, OK 74076.)

# APPENDIX 2

# Some Organizations Dealing with Junior Faculty Development

For further information, see the sections "Tactics for Developing Junior Faculty Scholarship," in chapter 5, and "Some Programs for Improving Junior Faculty Teaching," in chapter 6.

*British universities* have long provided development programs for junior faculty members. These are described in Peter Seldin's *Teaching Professors to Teach.*

The *Central Pennsylvania Consortium* consists of three small neighboring liberal arts colleges—Dickinson, Franklin and Marshall, and Gettysburg—that have joined to work on projects, of which junior faculty development is only one. The consortium is directed by Stephen C. MacDonald, Dickinson College, Carlisle, PA 17013; 717 245-1490. The junior faculty workshop is directed by Stanley Michalak, a professor of government at Franklin and Marshall. His home address is Box 276 RD 1, Bird-in-Hand, PA 17505.

The *Great Lakes Colleges Association*, a consortium of twelve liberal arts colleges near the Great Lakes, sponsors junior and senior faculty development programs, including an interinstitutional mentoring program pairing junior professors with senior colleagues outside the junior professors' institutions. The address and phone number of the association are Suite 207, 2929 Plymouth Rd., Ann Arbor, MI 48105-3206; 313 761-4833.

The *Joyce Foundation* has a strong interest in the development of teaching, particularly among small private colleges in the Midwest. Unlike the Lilly Endowment, which initiates projects itself and has well-defined guidelines, the Joyce Foundation will consider a variety of proposals from the field. The address and phone number of the foundation are 135 S. La Salle St., Chicago, IL 60603; 312 782-2464.

The *Lilly Endowment Post-doctoral Teaching Awards Program*, the largest program for junior faculty members, is briefly described in chapter 5. Participation is by invitation, and only public universities east of the Mississippi River are eligible. The address and phone number of the Lilly Endowment are 2801 N. Meridian St., P.O. Box 88068, Indianapolis, IN 46208-0068; 317 924-5471.

The *Professional and Organizational Development Network in Higher Education* is the main professional organization of development specialists in higher education. It holds an annual conference, publishes a yearbook, and produces a newsletter and other information touching the development of faculty members, including junior professors.

The Division of Instructional Development of the *University of Illinois* has organized ninety-minute seminars for new faculty members in each college and in various departments. Further information on this program is available from Marne Helgesen, the head, and Nancy A. Diamond, an education specialist, at the Division of Instructional Development, 307 Engineering Hall, 1308 W. Green St., Univ. of Illinois, Urbana, IL 61801.

The *University of Oklahoma* has a semester-long weekly seminar for new faculty members in the fall semester. Participants meet on a voluntary basis for lunch followed by a ninety-minute program focusing primarily on teaching and general orientation; a few sessions are devoted to research. For more information about the seminar, write or call the director, Dee Fink, Instructional Development Program, Room 116, Carnegie Bldg., Univ. of Oklahoma, Norman, OK 73019; 405 325-3521.

The *University of Texas at Austin* holds a teaching seminar for all new professors during the three days preceding fall registration. Further information on this program is available from the assistant director, Karron G. Lewis, Center for Teaching Effectiveness, Main Bldg. 2200, Univ. of Texas, Austin, TX 78712-1111; 512 471-1488.

# APPENDIX 3

# Interview Guide Used in the Survey of Academics

Professor: _____
University: _____
Profile: _____

(Ask questions marked with an asterisk [*] only if needed.)

1. What does the system reward at this university?

2. What would be an ideal reward system?

3. What is the present system of development for the junior faculty at this university?

4. What do you believe should be done to best develop young faculty members in the first decade after they are hired?

   *a. What can be done to encourage their general intellectual development? Can more be done to foster personal contacts and participation in the larger community of scholars?

5. Where and in what year did you complete your graduate work?

6. Could you briefly describe the institution(s) where you worked in the first five years after completing graduate work—your first real university position(s)?

   *a. What activities were rewarded?

7. How many hours per week did you usually work on university-related projects during your first five years? _____ How many contact hours did you spend in class with students each week? _____

8. Why are you successful? (What major factors or individuals have helped you develop as a professional?)

   a. Have there been any turning points in which your career clearly took a different direction?

9. Has anything or anyone hindered your development?

   a. Has your teaching helped or hindered your career?

   b. Has your administrative work helped or hindered your career?

10. *For scholars only:*
Can you briefly describe your strategies for research and publishing?

   \*a. How do you generate ideas?

   \*b. How do you plan and protect time for a research project?

   \*c. What sort of resources do you usually need, and how do you get them?

   \*d. What is your style of researching? (Do you take notes? If so, how do you record, arrange, and store them?)

   \*e. How do you get your research into publishable form?

   \*f. How do you select a publisher?

11. *For teachers only:*
Can you briefly describe your strategies for teaching?

   \*a. What advance planning do you do?

   \*b. How do you actually deliver your information to your students? (How much do you rely on lectures?)

   \*c. How do you arrange interaction with students?

   \*d. What is good teaching?

   \*e. Can teaching be evaluated? How?

12. *For administrators only:*
Why is this unit successful?

   \*a. How do you generate ideas?

   \*b. How far in advance do you like to plan?

   \*c. What sort of leadership style do you prefer? (Is your approach authoritarian, or do you try to build a consensus?)

13. Am I asking the right questions? What should I be asking about?

14. Do you have a curriculum vitae you could let me have?

# APPENDIX 4

# Results of the Survey of Academics

### Number Interviewed at Each Institution by Academic Group

| SCHOOL | TOTAL | SCHOLARS | TEACHERS | ADMIN. | JR. FAC. MEMBERS | WOMEN | MEN |
|---|---|---|---|---|---|---|---|
| Dickinson Coll. | 15 | 3 | 7 | 1 | 4 | 5 | 10 |
| Harvard Univ. | 7 | 5 | 1 | — | 1 | 2 | 5 |
| Stanford Univ. | 16 | 7 | 4 | 2 | 3 | 4 | 12 |
| Univ. of California at Santa Cruz | 16 | 5 | 3 | 4 | 4 | 5 | 11 |
| Univ. of Chicago | 18 | 8 | 4 | 3 | 3 | 4 | 14 |
| Univ. of Illinois at Chicago | 11 | 6 | 2 | 1 | 2 | 3 | 8 |
| Univ. of Maryland at College Park | 15 | 9 | 1 | 2 | 3 | 3 | 12 |
| Yale Univ. | 15 | 4 | 3 | 4 | 4 | 3 | 12 |
| Miscellaneous* | 4 | 1 | 1 | — | 2 | — | 4 |
| Total | 117 | 48 | 26 | 17 | 26 | 29 | 88 |
| Percentage of total | 100% | 41% | 22% | 15% | 22% | 25% | 75% |

*Two junior faculty members were interviewed at the Center for Hellenic Studies in Washington, DC, and two senior faculty members were interviewed at Brigham Young University.

## Table A
## Responses to Question 1 (What Does the System Reward at This University?), by Percentage of Academic Groups

| RESPONSE | TOTAL ($N=101$) | SCHOLARS ($N-41$) | TEACHERS ($N-23$) | ADMIN. ($N-15$) | JR. FAC. MEMBERS ($N=22$) | WOMEN ($N-24$) | MEN ($N-77$) |
|---|---|---|---|---|---|---|---|
| 1. Research primarily | 79 | 88 | 70 | 93 | 64 | 71 | 82 |
| a. With quality > quantity | 7 | 15 | — | 7 | — | 4 | 8 |
| b. With quality < quantity | 7 | 10 | 4 | 7 | 5 | 4 | 8 |
| c. With teaching or service counting some | 50 | 51 | 48 | 60 | 41 | 50 | 49 |
| d. With exceptional teaching sometimes rewarded, without much publication | 2 | 2 | 4 | — | — | — | 3 |
| 2. Teaching primarily | 15* | 5* | 30* | 13* | 18* | 21* | 13* |
| a. With research second, then service | 13* | 2* | 30* | 7* | 18* | 17* | 12* |
| 3. Both teaching & research | 5 | 2 | — | — | 18 | 8 | 4 |
| 4. Line admins. rewarded financially | 6 | 10 | — | 13 | — | 4 | 7 |
| 5. All three equally | 1 | 2 | — | — | — | — | 1 |
| 6. Outside offers | 3 | 2 | — | — | 9 | — | 4 |
| 7. Interdisciplinary teaching | 1 | 2 | — | — | — | — | 1 |
| 8. Nothing | 1 | 2 | — | — | — | 4 | — |
| 9. Not jr. fac. teachers—they are used & discarded | 2 | 2 | 4 | — | — | 4 | 1 |

This table provides the percentages of respondents in various groups giving the responses listed. $N =$ the number giving any response to this question. Most informants made several comments, so the percentages in each column usually add up to more than 100%. All percentages are rounded to the nearest whole percent.

---

*All these responses were from informants at Dickinson.

## Table B
### Responses to Question 2 (What Would Be an Ideal Reward System?), by Percentage of Academic Groups

| RESPONSE | TOTAL (N=106) | SCHOLARS (N=44) | TEACHERS (N=25) | ADMIN. (N=13) | JR. FAC. MEMBERS (N=24) | WOMEN (N=28) | MEN (N=78) |
|---|---|---|---|---|---|---|---|
| 1. Change is necessary | 83 | 80 | 88 | 77 | 88 | 89 | 81 |
| 2. Emphasize teaching or administration more | 69 | 52 | 84 | 77 | 79 | 79 | 65 |
| a. Reward teaching more | 56 | 43 | 72 | 54 | 63 | 57 | 55 |
| b. Reward service more | 18 | 16 | 16 | 23 | 21 | 14 | 19 |
| c. Use multiple tracks or emphases | 17 | 9 | 24 | 23 | 21 | 21 | 15 |
| d. Increase informal rewards* | 3 | — | 8 | 8 | — | 4 | 3 |
| e. Emphasize research quality | 5 | 7 | — | 15 | — | — | 6 |
| 3. Continue the research emphasis | 25 | 43 | 12 | 15 | 8 | 18 | 27 |
| a. Stress quality, not quantity (decrease pressure to publish) | 9 | 18 | 4 | 8 | — | 7 | 10 |
| b. Make tenure easier to obtain | 3 | 7 | — | — | — | — | 4 |
| c. Increase pay | 1 | 2 | — | — | — | — | 1 |
| d. Clarify signals | 2 | 2 | — | — | 4 | 4 | 1 |
| e. Use multiple emphases | 2 | 5 | — | — | — | 4 | 1 |
| 4. Miscellaneous | 10 | 2 | 4 | 23 | 25 | 18 | 8 |
| a. Be more explicit | 3 | 2 | — | — | 8 | — | 4 |
| b. Abolish tenure for senior faculty | 3 | — | — | 8 | 8 | 7 | 1 |
| c. Stress development over evaluation | 2 | — | — | 8 | 4 | 7 | — |

This table provides the percentages of respondents in various groups giving the responses listed. N = the number giving any response to this question. Most informants made several comments, so the percentages in each column usually add up to more than 100%. All percentages are rounded to the nearest whole percent.

*The heading "Increase informal rewards" includes responses that suggested increasing nonevaluative, informal interaction among faculty members by such means as colloquiums on teaching, more opportunities to visit classes, and so forth.

*Table C*
*Responses to Question 3 (What is the Present System of Development for the Junior Faculty at This University?), by Percentage of Academic Groups*

| RESPONSE | TOTAL (N=102) | SCHOLARS (N=42) | TEACHERS (N=23) | ADMIN. (N=13) | JR. FAC. MEMBERS (N=24) | WOMEN (N=25) | MEN (N=77) |
|---|---|---|---|---|---|---|---|
| 1. Resources: time, money, equipment | 75 | 71 | 83 | 77 | 71 | 76 | 74 |
| a. Time off from teaching | 43 | 43 | 44 | 62 | 33 | 32 | 47 |
| b. Sharing teaching and admin. loads fairly with the sr. fac. | 27 | 24 | 17 | 69 | 17 | 24 | 27 |
| c. Travel money | 20 | 17 | 13 | 31 | 25 | 32 | 16 |
| d. Complete or partial research funding | 44 | 41 | 48 | 39 | 50 | 44 | 44 |
| e. Institute for humanities | 11 | 10 | 4 | 23 | 13 | 8 | 12 |
| f. Teaching resources (video recording, student observers, etc.) | 9 | 10 | 17 | — | 4 | 12 | 8 |
| g. Curriculum development awards | 7 | — | 17 | 8 | 8 | 20 | 3 |
| h. Housing assistance | 3 | 5 | — | 8 | — | — | 4 |
| 2. Collegiality | 49 | 38 | 39 | 69 | 67 | 52 | 48 |
| a. Mentoring jr. fac. members | 4 | — | — | 8 | 13 | 4 | 4 |
| b. Fostering outside contacts (networking) | 2 | 5 | — | — | — | — | 3 |
| c. Involvement with the sr. fac. in teaching or research | 7 | 7 | 9 | 8 | 4 | — | 9 |
| d. Jr. fac. ideas heard with respect & trust | 15 | 17 | 9 | 8 | 21 | 12 | 16 |
| e. Sense of support or belonging | 19 | 10 | 9 | 31 | 38 | 28 | 16 |
| f. Feedback on strengths, weaknesses, expectations | 20 | 12 | 17 | 39 | 25 | 20 | 20 |
| g. Adequate time to make tenure | 3 | 2 | — | 15 | — | — | 4 |
| h. Intellectual exchange (informal) | 8 | 5 | 9 | 8 | 13 | 12 | 7 |

## Table C (cont.)

| RESPONSE | TOTAL (N=102) | SCHOLARS (N=42) | TEACHERS (N=23) | ADMIN. (N=13) | JR. FAC. MEMBERS (N=24) | WOMEN (N=25) | MEN (N=77) |
|---|---|---|---|---|---|---|---|
| 3. Training | 32 | 29 | 26 | 31 | 46 | 36 | 31 |
| a. Seminars, workshops, colloquiums | 28 | 26 | 17 | 31 | 38 | 24 | 29 |
| b. Interdisciplinary programs | 7 | 5 | 4 | — | 17 | 12 | 5 |
| c. Teaching in specialty or area of interest | 1 | — | 4 | — | — | 4 | — |
| 4. Hindrances to jr. fac. development | 27 | 33 | 26 | 8 | 25 | 28 | 26 |
| a. Not much help—sink or swim | 15 | 26 | 4 | — | 13 | 12 | 16 |
| b. This system hinders promotion & development | 16 | 14 | 22 | 8 | 17 | 24 | 13 |
| i. Heavy teaching & admin. loads hinder development | 6 | 5 | — | 8 | 13 | 4 | 6 |
| ii. Researchers' loads are too light | 1 | — | — | — | 4 | — | 1 |
| iii. Lack of collegiality | 7 | 2 | 17 | — | 8 | 12 | 5 |
| iv. Poor direction, support, feedback | 2 | — | 4 | — | 4 | — | 3 |
| v. Sexual or racial discrimination | 3 | 7 | — | — | — | 12 | — |

This table provides the percentages of respondents in various groups giving the responses listed. $N$ = the number giving any response to this question. Most informants made several comments, so the percentages in each column usually add up to more than 100%. All percentages are rounded to the nearest whole percent.

*Table D*
*Responses to Question 4 (What Do You Believe Should Be Done to Best Develop Young Faculty Members?), by Percentage of Academic Groups*

| RESPONSE | TOTAL (N=109) | SCHOLARS (N=44) | TEACHERS (N=26) | ADMIN. (N=15) | JR. FAC. MEMBERS (N=24) | WOMEN (N=27) | MEN (N=82) |
|---|---|---|---|---|---|---|---|
| 1. Resources: time, money, equipment | 76 | 80 | 65 | 80 | 79 | 81 | 74 |
| a. Time off from teaching | 37 | 48 | 27 | 33 | 33 | 37 | 38 |
| b. Reducing teaching and admin. or sharing with the sr. fac. | 29 | 32 | 23 | 40 | 25 | 26 | 30 |
| c. Travel money | 30 | 30 | 31 | 27 | 33 | 37 | 28 |
| d. Complete or partial research funding | 28 | 30 | 23 | 13 | 38 | 33 | 26 |
| e. Improved equipment or facilities | 16 | 9 | 19 | 13 | 25 | 26 | 12 |
| f. Help with grantsmanship | 6 | 9 | 8 | — | — | 7 | 5 |
| 2. Collegiality | 89 | 84 | 100 | 80 | 92 | 89 | 89 |
| a. Mentoring jr. fac. members | 31 | 34 | 31 | 40 | 21 | 37 | 29 |
| b. Fostering outside contacts (networking) | 23 | 11 | 23 | 33 | 38 | 33 | 20 |
| c. Involvement with the sr. fac. in teaching or research | 17 | 18 | 23 | 13 | 13 | 15 | 18 |
| d. Jr. fac. ideas heard with respect & trust | 17 | 14 | 19 | 20 | 21 | 22 | 16 |
| e. Sense of support or belonging | 32 | 27 | 27 | 40 | 42 | 48 | 27 |
| f. Feedback on strengths & weaknesses; clear explanation of tenure process | 24 | 23 | 23 | 20 | 29 | 33 | 21 |
| g. Fairer settlement of tenure (adequate time) | 11 | 14 | 15 | — | 8 | 11 | 11 |
| h. Intellectual exchange (informal) | 11 | 9 | 15 | — | 17 | — | 15 |
| i. Focus on development of potential & less on evaluation of past | 8 | 2 | 8 | 13 | 17 | 19 | 5 |

*Table D* (cont.)

| RESPONSE | TOTAL (N=109) | SCHOLARS (N=44) | TEACHERS (N=26) | ADMIN. (N=15) | JR. FAC. MEMBERS (N=24) | WOMEN (N=27) | MEN (N=82) |
|---|---|---|---|---|---|---|---|
| 3. Training | 61 | 48 | 65 | 60 | 79 | 74 | 56 |
| a. Colloquiums, workshops, seminars, etc. | 30 | 23 | 35 | 27 | 42 | 44 | 26 |
| b. Encouragement of teaching development & innovation; stimulation of colleagues | 32 | 25 | 35 | 40 | 38 | 33 | 32 |
| c. Writing across curriculum | 2 | — | 4 | 7 | — | 4 | 1 |
| d. Teaching in speciality or area of interest | 8 | 9 | 15 | — | 4 | 7 | 9 |
| e. Interdisciplinary seminar work | 6 | 2 | 8 | 13 | 8 | 11 | 5 |
| 4. Other | 9 | 11 | 4 | 13 | 8 | 15 | 7 |
| a. Better support for women and minorities | 7 | 11 | 4 | — | 8 | 15 | 5 |

This table provides the percentages of respondents in various groups giving the responses listed. $N =$ the number giving any response to this question. Most informants made several comments, so the percentages in each column usually add up to more than 100%. All percentages are rounded to the nearest whole percent.

*Table E*
**Responses to Question 8 (Why Are You Successful? [What Major Factors or Individuals Have Helped You Develop as a Professional?]), by Percentage of Academic Groups**

| RESPONSE | TOTAL (N=89) | SCHOLARS (N=46) | TEACHERS (N=23) | ADMIN. (N=8) | JR. FAC. MEMBERS (N=12) | WOMEN (N=19) | MEN (N=70) |
|---|---|---|---|---|---|---|---|
| 1. Resources | 36 | 50 | 17 | — | 42 | 26 | 39 |
| a. Leaves, grants, prizes | 31 | 44 | 17 | — | 33 | 21 | 34 |
| b. Access to good library | 2 | 2 | — | — | 8 | 5 | 1 |
| 2. Collegiality | 63 | 72 | 48 | 63 | 58 | 68 | 61 |
| a. Mentor or sponsor | 21 | 28 | 13 | 13 | 17 | 21 | 21 |
| b. Networking, contact with scholars, etc. | 20 | 24 | 13 | 13 | 25 | 26 | 19 |
| c. Advice & support of friends & colleagues | 25 | 26 | 17 | 13 | 42 | 37 | 21 |
| d. Family or spouse supportive | 13 | 22 | 4 | 13 | — | 16 | 13 |
| e. Good training & advice in grad. school | 9 | 9 | 13 | 13 | — | 11 | 9 |
| 3. Early development | 48 | 48 | 57 | 50 | 33 | 47 | 49 |
| a. Early publication | 24 | 24 | 22 | 13 | 33 | 26 | 23 |
| b. Involvement in project or dept. | 9 | 13 | 9 | — | — | 5 | 10 |
| c. Teaching | 9 | 4 | 22 | — | 8 | 5 | 10 |
| d. Admin. tasks | 10 | 13 | 9 | 13 | — | 11 | 10 |
| e. Luck | 12 | 15 | 9 | 25 | — | 5 | 14 |
| 4. Course of career | 69 | 76 | 70 | 63 | 42 | 53 | 73 |
| a. Broad background or change of scholarly focus | 37 | 41 | 39 | 38 | 17 | 26 | 40 |
| b. Opportunities at a university | 18 | 22 | 22 | — | 8 | 5 | 21 |
| c. Change of schools | 20 | 28 | 9 | 13 | 17 | 16 | 21 |
| d. Promotion to full professor | 1 | — | 4 | — | — | — | 1 |
| e. Admin. tasks | 3 | — | 4 | 25 | — | 5 | 3 |
| 5. Individual abilities or traits | 48 | 52 | 57 | 50 | 17 | 37 | 51 |
| a. Specific abilities or traits | 25 | 28 | 30 | 13 | 8 | 21 | 26 |
| b. Early experience (outside school) | 13 | 20 | 9 | 13 | — | 11 | 14 |
| c. Love of job | 6 | — | 9 | 13 | 17 | 5 | 6 |

## Table E (cont.)

| RESPONSE | TOTAL (N=89) | SCHOLARS (N=46) | TEACHERS (N=23) | ADMIN. (N=8) | JR. FAC. MEMBERS (N=12) | WOMEN (N=19) | MEN (N=70) |
|---|---|---|---|---|---|---|---|
| d. Hard work | 15 | 15 | 17 | — | 17 | 5 | 17 |
| e. Good organization | 4 | 4 | 9 | — | — | 5 | 4 |
| f. Patience, persistence, resilience | 4 | 4 | 4 | 13 | — | 5 | 4 |
| g. Individual experiences (e.g., sick spouse) | 3 | 2 | 4 | — | 8 | 11 | 1 |

This table provides the percentages of respondents in various groups giving the responses listed. $N =$ the number giving any response to this question. Most informants made several comments, so the percentages in each column usually add up to more than 100%. All percentages are rounded to the nearest whole percent.

## Table F
### Responses to Question 9 (Has Anything or Anyone Hindered Your Development?), by Percentage of Academic Groups

| RESPONSE | TOTAL (N=38) | SCHOLARS (N=19) | TEACHERS (N=10) | ADMIN. (N=4) | JR. FAC. MEMBERS (N=5) | WOMEN (N=9) | MEN (N=29) |
|---|---|---|---|---|---|---|---|
| 1. Lack of collegiality | 50 | 58 | 50 | 25 | 40 | 56 | 48 |
| a. Lack of encouragement or of achieving atmosphere | 24 | 32 | 20 | 25 | — | 22 | 24 |
| b. Lack of professional contacts | 11 | 11 | 10 | — | 20 | 11 | 10 |
| c. Lack of support for women or of women role models | 3 | — | — | — | 20 | 11 | — |
| d. Anti-Semitism or other discrimination | 5 | 11 | — | — | — | 11 | 3 |
| e. Conflicts with colleagues | 8 | 5 | 20 | — | — | — | 10 |
| 2. Competing professional interests | 13 | 11 | 20 | 25 | — | 11 | 14 |
| a. Admin. responsibilities | 5 | — | 20 | — | — | 11 | 3 |
| b. Letter writing for colleagues | 3 | 5 | — | — | — | — | 3 |
| c. Heavy course loads | 3 | 5 | — | — | — | — | 3 |
| d. Joint appointments | 3 | — | — | 25 | — | — | 3 |
| 3. Competing personal interests | 29 | 32 | 20 | — | 60 | 44 | 24 |
| a. Competing personal interests outside family | 5 | 11 | — | — | — | — | 7 |
| b. Competing family interests | 16 | 11 | 10 | — | 60 | 33 | 10 |
| c. Interrupted career | 5 | — | 10 | — | 20 | 22 | — |
| d. Miscellaneous | 8 | 16 | — | — | — | — | 10 |
| 4. Miscellaneous | 21 | 5 | 30 | 50 | 40 | 11 | 24 |
| a. Inadequate background or lack of preparation | 11 | 5 | 10 | 50 | — | 11 | 10 |
| b. Lack of money | 5 | — | 10 | — | 20 | — | 7 |
| c. Lack of facilities | 5 | — | 10 | — | 20 | — | 7 |

This table provides the percentages of respondents in various groups giving the responses listed. N = the number giving any response to this question. Most informants made several comments, so the percentages in each column usually add up to more than 100%. All percentages are rounded to the nearest whole percent.

## Table G
### Responses to Question 9a (Has Your Teaching Helped or Hindered Your Career?), by Percentage of Academics Groups

| RESPONSE | TOTAL (N=43) | SCHOLARS (N=25) | TEACHERS (N=8) | ADMIN. (N=3) | JR. FAC. MEMBERS (N=7) | WOMEN (N=8) | MEN (N=35) |
|---|---|---|---|---|---|---|---|
| 1. Stimulates growth, understanding, learning | 35 | 28 | 63 | 33 | 29 | 38 | 34 |
| 2. Enriches scholarly writing | 37 | 48 | 13 | 100 | 43 | 25 | 40 |
| 3. Generates ideas | 14 | 16 | 100 | 33 | 14 | 13 | 14 |
| 4. Helps when it doesn't overburden | 19 | 16 | 25 | 33 | 14 | 25 | 17 |

This table provides the percentages of respondents in various groups giving the responses listed. $N =$ the number giving any response to this question. Most informants made several comments, so the percentages in each column usually add up to more than 100%. All percentages are rounded to the nearest whole percent.

## Table H
### Responses to Question 9b (Has Your Administrative Work Helped or Hindered Your Career?), by Percentage of Academic Groups

| RESPONSE | TOTAL (N=41) | SCHOLARS (N=18) | TEACHERS (N=8) | ADMIN. (N=7) | JR. FAC. MEMBERS (N=8) | WOMEN (N=7) | MEN (N=34) |
|---|---|---|---|---|---|---|---|
| 1. Helped | 27 | 28 | 25 | 29 | 25 | 57 | 21 |
| 2. Hindered | 37 | 33 | 25 | 43 | 50 | 43 | 35 |
| 3. Neutral | 12 | 17 | 13 | — | 13 | — | 15 |
| 4. Don't like it | 12 | 17 | 25 | — | — | — | 15 |
| 5. Like it, or other positive responses | 20 | 11 | 25 | 29 | 25 | — | 24 |

This table provides the percentages of respondents in various groups giving the responses listed. $N =$ the number giving any response to this question. Most informants made several comments, so the percentages in each column usually add up to more than 100%. All percentages are rounded to the nearest whole percent.

## Table I
### Responses to Question 10a (How Do You Generate Ideas?), by Percentage of Academic Groups

| RESPONSE | TOTAL (N=43) | SCHOLARS (N=40) | TEACHERS (N=2) | ADMIN. (N=1) | JR. FAC. MEMBERS (N=0) | WOMEN (N=5) | MEN (N=38) |
|---|---|---|---|---|---|---|---|
| 1. Collegial exchange, personal contacts, professional meetings | 44 | 43 | 50 | 100 | — | 60 | 42 |
| 2. Reading (particularly primary sources) | 51 | 50 | 50 | 100 | — | 40 | 53 |
| 3. Preparing to teach, previous teaching, contact with students | 42 | 40 | 50 | 100 | — | 40 | 42 |
| 4. Critical thinking—asking & following up questions, going behind current ideas, updating | 35 | 38 | — | — | — | 40 | 34 |
| 5. Own writing & previous research projects | 16 | 18 | — | — | — | — | 18 |
| 6. Undertaking broad subjects, integrating diverse ideas | 21 | 23 | — | — | — | 20 | 21 |
| 7. Recording own ideas (keeping notebook, jotting ideas) | 12 | 13 | — | — | — | 20 | 11 |
| 8. Requests to write on specific topics | 14 | 15 | — | — | — | 20 | 13 |
| 9. Testing out ideas as papers | 7 | 8 | — | — | — | 20 | 5 |
| 10. Desire to communicate to general public; a sense of the practical, of real life, of "news" | 12 | 13 | — | — | — | 20 | 11 |
| 11. Exploring own interests | 12 | 13 | — | — | — | — | 13 |
| 12. Conversations with spouse | 5 | 5 | — | — | — | — | 5 |

This table provides the percentages of respondents in various groups giving the responses listed. $N$ = the number giving any response to this question. Most informants made several comments, so the percentages in each column usually add up to more than 100%. All percentages are rounded to the nearest whole percent.

*Table J*
## Responses to Question 10b (How Do You Plan and Protect Time for a Research Project?), by Percentage of Academic Groups

| RESPONSE | TOTAL (N=41) | SCHOLARS (N=36) | TEACHERS (N=4) | ADMIN. (N=1) | JR. FAC. MEMBERS (N=0) | WOMEN (N=5) | MEN (N=36) |
|---|---|---|---|---|---|---|---|
| 1. Able to use small blocks or fragments of time, certain days, parts of a day | 66 | 67 | 75 | — | — | 80 | 64 |
| a. Write first thing in the morning | 10 | 11 | — | — | — | 40 | 6 |
| b. Write principally 8 a.m.–6 p.m.; use evenings & weekends for class preparation | 2 | 3 | — | — | — | — | 3 |
| 2. Like larger blocks of time, leaves, etc. | 37 | 36 | 25 | 100 | — | 20 | 39 |
| 3. Work in response to outside pressure | 10 | 8 | 25 | — | — | — | 11 |

This table provides the percentages of respondents in various groups giving the responses listed. $N$ = the number giving any response to this question. Most informants made several comments, so the percentages in each column usually add up to more than 100%. All percentages are rounded to the nearest whole percent.

*Table K*
## Responses to Question 10c (What Sort of Resources Do You Usually Need, and How Do You Get Them?), by Percentage of Academic Groups

| RESPONSE | TOTAL ($N=32$) | SCHOLARS ($N=30$) | TEACHERS ($N=1$) | ADMIN. ($N=1$) | JR. FAC. MEMBERS ($N=0$) | WOMEN ($N=3$) | MEN ($N=29$) |
|---|---|---|---|---|---|---|---|
| 1. Research assistants | 16 | 17 | — | — | — | — | 17 |
| 2. Word processor | 38 | 37 | — | 100 | — | — | 41 |
| 3. Typists or secretary | 22 | 23 | — | — | — | — | 24 |
| 4. Books collected to have on hand | 3 | 3 | — | — | — | — | 3 |
| 5. Very few resources needed | 6 | 7 | — | — | — | — | 7 |
| 6. Grants | 9 | 10 | — | — | — | 33 | 7 |
| 7. Travel money | 19 | 20 | — | — | — | 33 | 17 |
| 8. Coauthor | 3 | 3 | — | — | — | — | 3 |
| 9. Pencil & yellow pad | 9 | 10 | — | — | — | 33 | 7 |
| 10. Papers circulated to attract feedback from others | 3 | 3 | — | — | — | — | 3 |
| 11. Library or archives | 16 | 13 | 100 | — | — | — | 17 |
| 12. Miscellaneous | 3 | 3 | — | — | — | — | 3 |

This table provides the percentages of respondents in various groups giving the responses listed. $N=$ the number giving any response to this question. Most informants made several comments, so the percentages in each column usually add up to more than 100%. All percentages are rounded to the nearest whole percent.

*Table L*
*Responses to Question 10d (What Is Your Style of Researching?), by Percentage of Academic Groups*

| RESPONSE | TOTAL (N=37) | SCHOLARS (N=35) | TEACHERS (N=2) | ADMIN. (N=0) | JR. FAC. MEMBERS (N=0) | WOMEN (N=5) | MEN (N=32) |
|---|---|---|---|---|---|---|---|
| 1. Take lots of notes | 62 | 66 | — | — | — | 60 | 63 |
| a. In notebooks or on sheets of paper | 24 | 26 | — | — | — | 40 | 22 |
| b. On cards | 16 | 17 | — | — | — | 20 | 16 |
| c. On a word processor | 5 | 6 | — | — | — | 20 | 3 |
| d. With careful organization | 22 | 23 | — | — | — | — | 25 |
| 2. Take few or no notes (keep most in head) | 38 | 37 | 50 | — | — | 20 | 41 |
| 3. Have haphazard or no organization for notes | 30 | 29 | 50 | — | — | 20 | 31 |
| 4. Use deductive approach—define main points early | 14 | 14 | — | — | — | — | 16 |
| 5. Use inductive approach—let main points emerge from reading | 16 | 17 | — | — | — | 20 | 16 |
| 6. Photocopy lots of material | 8 | 6 | 50 | — | — | — | 9 |
| 7. Try to collect the needed books to have on hand | 8 | 6 | 50 | — | — | 40 | 3 |

This table provides the percentages of respondents in various groups giving the responses listed. N = the number giving any response to this question. Most informants made several comments, so the percentages in each column usually add up to more than 100%. All percentages are rounded to the nearest whole percent.

*Table M*
## Responses to Question 10e (How Do You Get Your Research into Publishable Form?), by Percentage of Scholar Groups

| RESPONSE | SCHOLARS ($N=28$) | WOMEN ($N=3$) | MEN ($N=25$) |
|---|---|---|---|
| 1. Make rough draft(s) and rewrite | 46 | 67 | 44 |
| 2. Sort notes into parts or chapters | 39 | 33 | 40 |
| 3. Use a word processor | 25 | 33 | 24 |
| 4. Make an outline | 7 | — | 8 |
| 5. Write throughout research project | 11 | — | 12 |
| 6. Talk it out | 7 | — | 8 |
| 7. Rely on memory | 7 | — | 8 |
| 8. Write backward—establish conclusions first | 4 | — | 4 |

This table provides the percentages of respondents in various groups giving the responses listed. $N =$ the number giving any response to this question. Most informants made several comments, so the percentages in each column usually add up to more than 100%. All percentages are rounded to the nearest whole percent.

*Table N*
### Responses to Question 10f (How Do You Select a Publisher?), by Percentage of Academic Groups

| RESPONSE | TOTAL (N=35) | SCHOLARS (N=33) | TEACHERS (N=1) | ADMIN. (N=1) | JR. FAC. MEMBERS (N=0) | WOMEN (N=3) | MEN (N=32) |
|---|---|---|---|---|---|---|---|
| 1. First consider academic or scholarly publishers | 31 | 33 | — | — | — | 67 | 28 |
| 2. Go for big, prestigious, commercial publishers first | 9 | 9 | — | — | — | 33 | 6 |
| 3. Use contacts & get advice | 34 | 36 | — | — | — | 33 | 34 |
| 4. Select appropriate publishers in area of research | 29 | 30 | — | — | — | 67 | 25 |
| 5. Submit to several publishers & keep trying when rejected | 31 | 30 | 100 | — | — | 100 | 25 |
| 6. Choose helpful publishers | 11 | 12 | — | — | — | — | 13 |
| 7. Stick with one publisher | 6 | 6 | — | — | — | — | 6 |
| 8. Am approached by publishers | 9 | 6 | — | 100 | — | — | 9 |
| 9. Concentrate more on articles | 26 | 27 | — | — | — | 33 | 25 |
| 10. Concentrate more on books | 17 | 18 | — | — | — | 33 | 16 |
| 11. Send letter of inquiry with outline or abstract | 9 | 9 | — | — | — | 33 | 6 |

This table provides the percentages of respondents in various groups giving the responses listed. $N$ = the number giving any response to this question. Most informants made several comments, so the percentages in each column usually add up to more than 100%. All percentages are rounded to the nearest whole percent.

*Table O*
*Responses to Question 11d (What Is Good Teaching?), by Percentage of Academic Groups*

| RESPONSE | TOTAL (N=35) | SCHOLARS (N=4) | TEACHERS (N=15) | ADMIN. (N=3) | JR. FAC. MEMBERS (N=13) | WOMEN (N=15) | MEN (N=20) |
|---|---|---|---|---|---|---|---|
| 1. Sparking student interest & participation | 51 | 50 | 68 | 67 | 31 | 60 | 45 |
| 2. Conveying critical thinking skills & a style of inquiry that enable students to learn on own | 46 | 25 | 40 | 100 | 46 | 47 | 45 |
| 3. Showing interest in & enthusiasm about subject; being excited | 23 | 50 | 27 | — | 15 | 7 | 35 |
| 4. Being interested in students | 14 | — | 7 | 33 | 23 | 27 | 5 |
| 5. Conveying knowledge & information clearly | 20 | — | 33 | — | 15 | 7 | 30 |
| 6. Being organized | 11 | 25 | 13 | — | 8 | 13 | 10 |
| 7. Conveying significance of subject | 14 | 50 | 13 | — | 8 | 7 | 20 |
| 8. Miscellaneous | 11 | 25 | 13 | — | 8 | 7 | 15 |

This table provides the percentages of respondents in various groups giving the responses listed. $N =$ the number giving any response to this question. Most informants made several comments, so the percentages in each column usually add up to more than 100%. All percentages are rounded to the nearest whole percent.

*Table P*
*Responses to Question 11e (Can Teaching Be Evaluated? How?), by
Percentage of Academic Groups*

| RESPONSE | TOTAL (N=24) | SCHOLARS (N=0) | TEACHERS (N=11) | ADMIN. (N=2) | JR. FAC. MEMBERS (N=11) | WOMEN (N=9) | MEN (N=15) |
|---|---|---|---|---|---|---|---|
| 1. Use objective student evaluations | 63 | — | 46 | 100 | 73 | 67 | 60 |
| 2. Minimize role of student evaluations or don't use them | 17 | — | 27 | — | 9 | 11 | 20 |
| 3. Use class visitations by colleagues or other peer evaluations | 63 | — | 64 | 100 | 55 | 33 | 80 |
| 4. Don't use class visitations by colleagues or other peer evaluations | 8 | — | 9 | — | 9 | — | 13 |
| 5. Examine course materials or content | 29 | — | 18 | 50 | 36 | 33 | 27 |
| 6. Don't consider course materials or content | 4 | — | — | — | 9 | — | 7 |
| 7. Use post hoc student evaluations | 17 | — | 18 | — | 18 | 22 | 13 |
| 8. Post hoc student evaluations aren't useful | 8 | — | 9 | 50 | — | 11 | 7 |
| 9. Use self-evaluation | 17 | — | 18 | — | 18 | 11 | 20 |
| 10. Use student evaluation in essay form | 29 | — | 18 | — | 46 | 33 | 27 |
| 11. Use graduating seniors' evaluations | 17 | — | 18 | 50 | 9 | 11 | 20 |
| 12. Use graduate students' evaluations | 4 | — | 9 | — | — | — | 7 |
| 13. Miscellaneous | 17 | — | 9 | — | 27 | 22 | 13 |

This table provides the percentages of respondents in various groups giving the responses listed. $N$ = the number giving any response to this question. Most informants made several comments, so the percentages in each column usually add up to more than 100%. All percentages are rounded to the nearest whole percent.

## Table Q
### Responses to Question 12 (Why Is This Unit Successful?), by Percentage of Administrative Groups

| RESPONSE | ADMIN. (*N*=10) | WOMEN (*N*=1) | MEN (*N*=9) |
|---|---|---|---|
| 1. Atmosphere of support, cooperation, & collegiality | 60 | — | 67 |
| 2. Obtaining quality people | 40 | — | 44 |
| 3. Flexibility—tolerance of a variety of views | 40 | — | 44 |
| 4. Consensus-identifying style of leadership | 40 | — | 44 |
| 5. Authoritarian style of leadership | 40 | 100 | 33 |
| 6. 5-year plans or long-term strategy | 20 | — | 22 |
| 7. Interdisciplinary education & training | 20 | — | 22 |
| 8. Miscellaneous | 20 | — | 22 |

This table provides the percentages of respondents in various groups giving the responses listed. *N* = the number giving any response to this question. Most informants made several comments, so the percentages in each column usually add up to more than 100%. All percentages are rounded to the nearest whole percent.

# INDEX